# Worship without Dumbing-down

## Knowing God through Liturgy

## by Peter Toon

Preservation Press of the
Prayer Book Society of the USA
and
Edgeways Books
2005

First published in this form in 2005 by
**The Preservation Press of the Prayer Book Society, USA**
P.O. Box 35220, Philadelphia, PA 19128-0220.
www.episcopalian.org/pbs1928

and in the United Kingdom by
**Edgeways Books**
6 Greencroft Avenue, Corbridge, Northumberland NE45 5DW England
www.edgewaysbooks.com

Designed and typeset by
Boldface Graphics—Houston, Texas

Printed in the USA

1-879793-05-9 (USA)
0-907839-90-8 (UK)

# CONTENTS

For
Louis R. Tarsitano,
Teacher of the Anglican Way, and Priest in the Church of God

# PREFACE

There is at least one generation of Episcopalians in the USA which has never attended or participated in a dynamic, traditional Anglican Liturgy, where God is addressed as "Thou," where the content is reformed Catholic doctrine, where the style of language is attractive to mind, heart, and ear, and where the music raises the affections towards heaven. There are also not a few persons, under say forty-five years of age, who are searching for a satisfying way of worship and who have not also experienced the spiritual, moral, and intellectual satisfaction of sharing in a classic, traditional Anglican liturgy. I hope this book, which commends and explains such liturgy, will be read by interested people in both these categories, as well, of course, by others of all ages and backgrounds.

I need to make clear that this book is not wholly new. It is a much revised and updated version of a book published in 1992 under the title, *Knowing God through the Liturgy* (Prayer Book Society, USA). I wrote that book, two years after my arrival in the USA from England, and when I was professor of systematic theology at Nashotah House Episcopal Seminary in Wisconsin. It arose in part out of my experience as an English priest seeking to live and serve within the Episcopal Church of the USA. I realized that this Church had discarded its traditional and inherited public Liturgy (*The Book of Common Prayer*, 1928) in favor of a new type of public Liturgy, a collection of varied services, which, most regrettably, it chose also to call, "*The Book of Common Prayer*" (1979).

Having been raised on the classic 1662 edition of *The Book of Common Prayer* in the Church of England, I was amazed to find that in the Episcopal Church and its seminaries the use of the American edition (1928) of this great English Liturgy was forbidden. I discovered that it was only used here and there in courageous parishes of the Episcopal Church, and by those Anglican congregations which had left the Episcopal Church and are often called "Continuing Anglicans." Therefore, I decided to write *Knowing God through the Liturgy*, where liturgy meant very particularly the historic, Anglican Liturgy that we know as *The Book of Common Prayer* in editions from 1549 through 1962. And this meant that I excluded the Episcopal Church's book of 1979 as a genuine *Book of Common Prayer*, since it is clearly a book of varied and alternative services, such as *The Alternative Service Book* (1980) of the Church of England.

Since 1992 it has become increasingly clearer to some of us that the Episcopal Church made a horrendous mistake in setting aside her inherited

Liturgy and making her new book of varied services (which is now judged by the General Convention to be out of date and in need of total renewal) into her official Prayer Book and doctrinal Formulary. It may be suggested that it is no accident of history that the Church, which abandoned its classic Liturgy and Formulary and much of its orthodox doctrine, worship, and discipline in the 1970s is, in the first decade of the twenty-first century, pursuing all kinds of questionable innovations in worship, doctrine, and practice, and is under severe censure from most of the Anglican family of Churches around the world.

So, I invite my reader, Anglican or other, to come with me on a journey and pilgrimage into the classic *Book of Common Prayer* (as we also carry the Bible in a traditional translation/version with us) in order to discover, or perhaps for some to confirm, how we come to know God, the living God, as the people of God and as disciples of the Lord Jesus Christ, through the faithful use of the reformed catholic Liturgy. The edition we use will be the American of 1928; but what we discover will also be applicable to the English edition of 1662 and the Canadian of 1962.

If I were asked for a biblical text to set forth what I desire to say, I would choose the word of the Lord through the prophet, Jeremiah. "Stand ye in the ways, and see, and ask for the old paths, where is the good way, and walk therein, and ye shall find rest for your souls" (6:16).

I invite my readers to choose the old way, not to bury their heads in the sands of the past, but with the intention of working to see its perfection for the Anglican Way for today and tomorrow. For, in the present way upon which Episcopal and Anglican provinces in the West are traveling, I do not see any long-term "rest for souls" or any real possibility of growth in quality of worship or numbers of members. In fact, I see the very opposite, the creation of a marginalized sect!

One final word. I heartily and resolutely dedicate this book to Louis Tarsitano, who died in Savannah, Georgia, in January 2005, at the age of fifty-three, with his faith and trust solidly based on our Lord Jesus Christ. He was an excellent apologist for the Anglican Way. With him, I had the privilege of working on many projects and writing five books, the two latest being, *Neither Archaic Nor Obsolete* and *Neither Orthodoxy Nor A Formulary*. His wisdom and gifts are deeply appreciated and greatly missed by many of us. In closing, may I say that the presentation of the logic and style of language for worship that we set forth in *Neither Archaic Nor Obsolete* is presupposed in the presentation of liturgy in this book?

Peter Toon, Trinity Sunday, 2005

# Worship without Dumbing-down

# THE AMERICAN EXPERIENCE

W hile the theme of this book is not unique, it is rare in the twenty-first century and in the West. To know God "one on One," to have a "personal relationship" with God, to cultivate individual spirituality, and to discover the inner self as an aspect of the universal Self, are popular themes for liberal and conservative alike, and for both Protestant and Catholic. Further, there is much use of the word "community" and the expression "Christian community" to describe the Christian assembly, gathered for worship and service.

However, to know the living God as a congregation, a fellowship, a flock of Christ, the household of God and the Body of Christ, is a topic not often discussed, described, or commended. Not that the corporate dimension eliminates the personal, but there is such a thing as a genuine corporate knowing of God. For in biblical logic the starting point is the corporate, the fellowship of the regenerate, the elect, the old and new Israel: and the personal comes to fruition and fulfillment therein. After all, it is from within holy, mother Church, not outside of her, that children of God are born from above by Water, the Word and the Holy Ghost!

## DUMBING-DOWN

Let me make a strong, perhaps controversial, assertion to set our thinking in motion. Worship of God, our Creator, Redeemer and Judge, is certainly dumbed-down in many American congregations each Sunday. To state this is only to be true to the facts as they are available for all to see, either by watching TV or visiting. Further, to assert this is to make a judgment. It is to recall earlier times when the content of worship was in general appreciably "higher" and its demands "more exacting." I recognize that those who are familiar only with the modern situation cannot meaningfully speak of dumbing-down, for they are not in a position to make a comparison with anything different, unless they visit other churches more traditional than their own on a regular basis, and thereby gain perspective.

What is presented and offered—often with the help of sophisticated technology—in a lot of American "worship services" today is a form of public words, music and action in a prepared context that is, as a whole, intended to be immediately appealing, relevant, simple, attractive, persuasive, and entertaining to the those present. The leadership and the gathered people know or sense this, and so they all plan and function accordingly. They seem to have the idea that to get people together in the name of God for recognition of God in prayer and thanksgiving, and to do so in a way that is not boring or demanding, but exciting and attractive, is a good thing in itself. Better for people to come before God in a simplified and attractive way, than not to come at all, appears to be a basic rule.

Whether the assembly is in a traditional parish adapting and simplifying a set liturgy, a community church creating its own local style of service, an inter-denominational church using a mixture of contents from a variety of traditions, or any another kind, those who attend are hardly there for "high" purposes. In fact, by the way they dress, one could deduce that they are engaging in what may be called a religious leisure activity. They are most probably there not in the first place to extend their horizons, not to cultivate a spiritual and heavenly mindset, not to be challenged by the Word of the living God, not to ponder the nature and attributes of God, not to see the depth and magnitude of their sins and the astounding and abundant mercy of God in Christ Jesus towards them, and not to be called to consecrated living day by day in the fear and love of the Lord. But, rather, they are there to satisfy some kind of spiritual or moral curiosity, need, searching, desiring, spiritual yearning or guilt. They are there to be affirmed, to be accepted, to feel and know their self-worth, and to recognize that they are God's children.

Having said this, I am not asserting that in these congregations there is no attempt to lead the people into a deepening appreciation and expression of Christian faith and life. Rather, it is to suggest that what is actually said and done, what is aimed at, called for, and expected of most people present is actually a minimum. That is, a minimum in terms of what could possibly be aimed at from within the rich content of the historic Christian tradition of conversion, worship, doctrine, discipline, morals, music, and lifestyle. In fact, it seems to be the case that worship, music, teaching, and discipline are deliberately and unashamedly dumbed-down, because it is believed that what people need, and can benefit from quickly, is really and truly a simplified, attractive, relevant, and plausible form of worship and discipleship. And, when one ponders the situation, this is not surprising, for we live in a culture wherein we eat fast and prepared (frozen) food, have current affairs and politics reduced for us to sound-bites and brief, vivid images, possess many gadgets to make doing anything as simple as possible, use only a very limited amount of the rich vocabulary of the English language, do not take the history of any people or any thing very seriously, have simplistic ideas of what genuine freedom is in any given country, and so on.

One very commonly-used word can and often does point to the dumbing-down of a very basic doctrinal matter—what God is to man and how man thinks of God. This word is used not only by those who dumb-down, but also by others who claim to be seriously liberal or orthodox, for it is a word that is over-used (to put it mildly) in modern English and has been adopted by religious discourse. It is the word, "relationship," which is a word not found in the classic versions of the English Bible or in *The Book of Common Prayer*, and very little used until the 1960s. It is probable that most people in earlier times went through life without ever using the word.

A "relationship," in contemporary usage, seems to be any kind of being together, coming together, or working together of two or more people or units of people that is based on voluntary association. That is, one party in this arrangement can break it at will, and then the "relationship" is no more. It is used often today of sexual associations, be they of heterosexual or homosexual persons, and be they covenants of marriage or other forms of living together. So when the word is used of the union of the believer with the Lord Jesus, the union of the believer with other believers in the Body of Christ, and the union of the whole Body of baptized, regenerate believers with the one Lord Jesus Christ, the Head, it suggests and contains ideas that are contrary to the Biblical teaching, as we shall see in later chapters. It suggests, for example, that everything is voluntary, can be started or ended at any time, and is of a low-level and of temporary association. How often does one hear on TV or radio words like these: "If you want a relationship with God, call this 1-800 number"!

We may note that the word "relation" is a better word to use for the union between Christ and his Church, as also between God the Father and a baptized believer and between the wife and husband in holy matrimony. This is because the word "relation" has a long and sacred history of use relating to permanent unions and associations, be it that of the Persons of the Holy Trinity, or persons in families, where relatives through blood and marriage are for ever, or at least for this life on earth.

We may recall that adding the suffix "ship" to the end of a noun changes its meaning to denote the state or condition of being what is expressed by the original noun. For example, "friendship" is the state or condition of being a friend; and it is an abstract word since it expresses the idea of being a friend. "Relationship" expresses the experience of a relation, not the concrete reality of being related—the real, lasting connection between persons.

So to emphasize "relationship" when speaking of union with God the Father or the Lord Jesus Christ is to stress our own understanding of what God has done, and is doing, over the very reality itself. To depend on our own ideas of "relationship" is to ask God to submit to us, rather than for us to submit to God the Father in the actual relation that he graciously gives us to the Lord Jesus Christ in the Gospel, on his terms alone by the Holy Ghost. It hardly needs to be stated that in a culture of personal, individual rights and of self-worth and self-realization, the tendency before God is to think and act as if one has rights and self-worth before the searching light of his holiness.

The classic teaching of the Church is this. There is an eternal, infinite relation of love between the Persons of the Trinity, the Father, the Son and the Holy Ghost. And God the Father by God the Holy Ghost creates a dynamic, eternal relation between believing sinners and the Incarnate Son, even our Lord Jesus Christ, so that through, by, in, and with Christ they may know God unto eternal life. Thus the Church of God, and all members thereof, have a relation by grace and mercy alone with the Father, through the Son and with the Holy Ghost: and, further, in fellowship, they are related one to another as members of Christ, who is their Head. We shall consider these truths in more detail in chapter four, when we discuss the covenant of grace.

Apart from the use of the word "relationship" there is also the use of the word, "community," for the assembled people of God. Strictly speaking, to describe the local church, the congregation of Christ's flock, as "a Christian community" is to speak in a way that hardly fits with the biblical doctrine and presentation of the union of believers in Christ by the Holy Ghost. Again this word does not occur in the classic translations of the Bible or in the historic *Book of Common Prayer*. The normal words used of the relation in the Body of Christ and Household of God of baptized believers are "communion" and "fellowship" (from the Greek word *koinonia* and the Latin word *communio*). The Church is made up of persons in communion with the Lord Jesus Christ and also with one another in him. They are also his sheep/flock, his soldiers/army and his disciples/school.

Modern use of the word "community," especially since the 1960s, presupposes the idea that "individuals" come together in a voluntary way to form an association on terms that all who come accept or negotiate. So first there are "individuals," and then there are "relationships," and then there is a "community," created by the acts of will of "individuals." And this is how many churches with a popular appeal appear to think and teach. Each one is "a community of individuals." Further, there is a tendency for this "Christian community" to seek to make all "individuals" conform to one standard and expression, set by the "inner community" of leaders—after all one major, older use of "community" stressed likeness, such as in a "Jewish" or "Polish" or "Irish" community.

The social philosopher, Robert Nisbet, describes "community" in this way: "Relationships among individuals that are characterized by a high degree of personal intimacy, of social cohesion or moral commitment, and of continuity in time. The basis of community may be kinship, religion, political power, revolution or race. It may be, in fact, any of a large number of activities, beliefs, or functions. All that is essential is that the basis be of sufficient appeal and of sufficient durability to enlist numbers of human beings, to arouse loyalties and to stimulate an over-riding sense of distinctive identity" (*The Social Philosophers: Community and Conflict*, New York, 1972, p. 1). In contrast, it may be recalled that a biblical picture of the local *ecclesia* of God is of the body which has many members, as different as foot from hand and stomach from heart, but with one Head, and all united in a common purpose, guided by the Head.

In contrast to thinking in terms of "individuals" and "community," the biblical way begins with Jesus Christ, as the One Person who is both God and Man, and who as the Man is "Man for others," the second Adam, the new Israel. In him, as the corporate Person, is salvation and life, and persons are drawn by the call of the Gospel and the power of the Holy Ghost into union and fellowship with him; and in being so placed, they gain, automatically, brothers and sisters in Christ. Thus the local assembly is not a modern voluntary community but a fellowship and communion, the coming together under Christ as Head of those who are already brothers and sisters in Christ. And those who come are individual persons (not merely "individuals"), who are made in the image and after the likeness of God, and who find no rest for their souls until they rest in the arms of the Lord Jesus Christ. The meeting of baptized Christians locally is not to create by their coming "a Christian community," but it is to experience by the grace of God what they already are through, by, in, and with Christ, their Head, the household of God, the communion of the faithful. [Historically, "community" is used of a convent or monastery, which with its permanent residents and property is like a village community; however, when its residents are at Mass they are not so much the community but the communion/fellowship. Regrettably in Roman Catholic writing this particular use of "community" has been generalized to refer to the church as a gathered assembly.]

# REFLECTION

Let us stop for a moment and ponder.

If there is a God; if this one God is the Creator, Redeemer and Judge of the world; and if this God is the Holy Trinity of the Father, the Son and the Holy Ghost, then it surely follows that any nation or tribe or person who does not seek to know and serve this Deity is not only foolish but also endangering life and soul.

The belief, confession and teaching of the one, holy, catholic and apostolic Church is precisely that there is One God, the LORD, and that he is a Trinity of Persons. This is declared in Creeds, Confessions of Faith and public Liturgies. Thus the vocation of the Church is to believe and trust, to worship and adore, to obey and serve, the Father, through the Son and with the Holy Ghost. Further, the Church as the Household of God, the Father, and as the Bride of Christ Jesus, the Son, is called to know God, the LORD, both in terms of knowing about him (his nature, attributes, character and revelation) and also, and very importantly, in terms of knowing him personally in terms of friendship, communion and fellowship. And knowing the Lord our God, the Church is to share her knowledge with the world in evangelization and service, guided by her Lord and indwelt by his Spirit.

This book seeks to provide advice and encouragement on a topic of great importance—how to know God the Holy Trinity within the Church, and particularly through the Liturgy, that is, in and through corporate worship using the services of *The Book of Common Prayer* in one or another of its classic editions. Of course, there is also a most important dimension for disciples of Christ Jesus of knowing God individually and personally in private devotion, Christian discipleship and vocation, that is, the knowing of the Person of the Father through the Person of the Son, the Mediator, and by the Presence of the Person of the Holy Ghost, the Counselor.

Experience and common sense, however, teach us that it is not possible to separate the personal from the corporate in Christian living, for all baptized Christians are members of the one Body of Christ and thus members one of another as they are also related through Christ to the Father. This recognized and said, in this book the primary concern will be with the congregation of Christ's flock as a fellowship in the Holy Ghost, as the Body of Christ indwelt by the same Spirit, seeking to know the Father in worship that is both "in spirit and in truth" and also in "the beauty of holiness."

Our God is the LORD, and we are made in his image and after his likeness to be his adoring creatures not only in this age but for all eternity. Therefore to begin to know him now in corporate worship is to prepare to know and serve him in heaven in the corporate Liturgy of the angels and saints.

## GOD DOES NOT FAVOR DUMBING-DOWN

We can be sure that the Holy Trinity does not favor dumbing-down because there is no evidence of it in the books of the Old and New Testaments, which contain the revelation of God to man. Certainly there is evidence of God addressing human beings in such a way as to make clear in relatively simple terms what he wants them to be and to do. But there is no evidence of the Word of the Lord being simplistic. If we look at the content of the Hebrew Old Testament and the Greek New Testament, we will not find anything that approaches the simplistic. Even in those far-off days, when there were no telephones or automobiles and very few people were educated in liberal arts, God addressed people as mature persons, respecting their God-given souls (minds, hearts, and wills).

God condescended to visit his creatures in space and time and to address them as sinful beings, yet as creatures made in his image and after his likeness. His Word to them demanded their full attention and called for the total exercise of their minds, hearts, and wills. Further, that Word usually came with levels of meaning so that people of varying maturity and discernment could immediately benefit from it and know that there was always much more to understand and make their own. In his call to human beings, God never looked for only a minimum understanding, appreciation and commitment. His call was, "Be holy as I am holy," and "Be perfect as I am perfect." He looked for and expected an ever increasing potential to hear, receive, understand and obey his word, so that his people could and would love him with all their heart, soul, mind, and strength!

To study the Gospels and the way that Jesus related to and taught his disciples is very illuminating in this respect. At one level, he seems to be telling simple stories about sheep and shepherds, farmers and laborers, trees and their fruit, and so on. Yet attached to the story are words such as, "The kingdom of heaven is like ... " Hearers are thus invited to think deeply, to make moral judgments, to see things from God's viewpoint, and to become committed members of the heavenly kingdom.

In his Epistles, St. Paul does not write so that he appeals to the lowest common denominator in the churches. He writes to the leaders (elders) of the churches in ways that they will be able to understand, and he expects them to read out and to explain his Epistle to the membership.

In fact the Bible is not an easy book to understand on first reading, even on the fifth reading! Those who claim to translate the Bible and simplify it for various target readerships, from children to busy commuters, do not necessarily do a favor to children or commuters! For the genuine believer, the way into the Bible gets more difficult, and yet more satisfying, the farther one enters. Points of entry and the circumference may be said to be relatively easy to understand, but that is not so as one continues along the holy road into the depth of the written Word. Understanding is related to deepening communion with God and obedience of his will, and cannot proceed without the illumination of the Holy Ghost.

So it is also with the use of *The Book of Common Prayer*, whose content is primarily portions of, and citations from, sacred Scripture. This reformed, catholic Liturgy was prepared initially for a whole nation, that of England, for use in its national Church, the Church of England. It was to be used by monarch and peasant, sailor and soldier, judge and student, mother and father, each of whom would grow into it through usage and good intention. It was accessible to all and could be appreciated by all and by each at his own level of maturity, discernment, and commitment. And, as used in the USA, first in colonial times, and since those years, this Prayer Book has had the same role and function, being there for all kinds and types of people to use at their level of maturity and experience.

## WISDOM FROM YESTERDAY

In their expositions of the traditional Anglican worship, many Anglicans from Richard Hooker to C. S. Lewis have made the point that worshippers are able to give themselves wholly to their high calling when they are using week by week the same, near-perfect expressions for praise and petition. They know always what is coming next and so are not disturbed or shaken in their concentration upon God through the act of worship. Further, it has always been the position of Anglican writers that the Anglican Way does not despise free and *ex tempore* forms of worship, including those of the modern charismatic movement, but that it considers that informal prayer meetings and Bible study groups are a more appropriate setting for them. Set forms in the best style of English are particularly suited to permanent and universal themes, whereas free prayer is more suited to occasional and individual themes and needs. And being of set form, liturgy can unite across space and through time.

Writing in the seventeenth century William Beveridge, Bishop of St Asaph, explained the difference for devotion between set prayer and *ex tempore* prayer. What he wrote also applies to modern dumbed-down and mix-and-match, ever-changing liturgy:

> Moreover, that which conduceth to the quickening of our souls and to the raising of our affections must needs be acknowledged to conduce much to edification. But it is plain that for such purposes a set form of prayer is an extraordinary help to us. For, if I hear another pray and know not beforehand what he will say, I must first listen to what he will say next: then I am to consider whether what he saith be agreeable to sound doctrine, and whether it be proper and lawful for me to join with him in the petitions he puts up to God Almighty: and if I think it is so, then I am to do it. But before I can well do that, he is got to another thing; by which means it is very difficult, if not morally impossible, to join with him in everything so regularly as I ought to do. But by a set form of prayer all this trouble is prevented; for having the form continually in my mind, being thoroughly acquainted with it, fully approving of everything in it, and always knowing beforehand what will come next, I have nothing else to do, whilst the words are sounding in mine ears, but to move my heart and affections suitably to them, to raise up my desires of those good things which are prayed for, to fix my mind wholly upon God whilst I am praising of him, and so to employ, quicken and lift up my soul in performing my devotions to him. No man that hath been accustomed to a set form for any considerable time, but may easily find this to be true by his own experience, and, by consequence, that this way of praying is a greater help to us than they can imagine that never made trial of it (*A Sermon on the Excellency of the Common Prayer*, 1681).

These are wise words, and had ministers and priests given explanations like this to young people, there would have been and remain today a greater understanding and deeper commitment to the Common Prayer Tradition. Divine service is not the place for experiment or for leaders to share their latest liturgical fads and fancies. It is the meeting with Almighty God, who calls us into his presence as his covenant people in the name of the Lord Jesus Christ. To gain fully from this encounter we need the most excellent form of words available to us.

In the next chapter, we shall examine what is called The Common Prayer Tradition in order to see what it is and where it is found today. With this task accomplished, we shall be free in chapter three to ask the question, "What is it to know God?"

Each of us probably knows a family which has recently gone through a major upheaval or crisis—be it a move from one place to another, the tragic death of a family member through death, a shattering divorce, or a great reduction of income. Yet how many of us know of a family which systematically planned to remove from its life together the actual means which gave it is historical identity and continuity, and which kept it together in a meaningful way? In terms of the Church as the family of God, then it is regrettably true of the Episcopal Church, and members and onlookers have witnessed this deliberate rejection of its heritage over the last thirty or more years. One major part of this rejection is of genuine, Anglican Common Prayer.

The Common Prayer Tradition in its English form began in 1549 with the publication of *The Book of the Common Prayer*. It had been known in Latin for centuries before 1549; but, from this date it was embodied in a revised and simplified form in several editions of the English Prayer Book (e.g., in 1662), with later revised editions in the English-speaking world of the British Empire, and the nations which evolved from it. There were, of course, many editions in foreign languages as well, especially for churches founded by missionary endeavor. In North America the first revised edition was in 1789 after the gaining of Independence by the colonies, and the last revised editions which truly embody this Common Prayer Tradition were those of 1928 in the USA and 1962 in Canada. Because of this shared tradition of common prayer amongst Anglicans world-wide, it was possible until fairly recently to go to Anglican worship anywhere in the world and soon feel at home with the forms of divine service. The sharing of the one *Book of Common Prayer* was the glue that bound the Anglican Churches around the world to each other in common worship.

The claim made by the standard divines of the Church of England from the end of the sixteenth century was this: that the reformed Catholic Faith is found stated in the official Formularies (Prayer Book, Articles of Religion and Ordinal), which are solidly based upon the standards of the Early Church. One distinguished divine, Lancelot Andrewes, expressed it in this way: "One Canon [of Scripture], reduced to writing by God himself, two Testaments [Old & New], Three Creeds [Apostles', Nicene, and Athanasian], four General Councils [Nicea, 325: Constantinople, 381; Ephesus, 431; and Chalcedon, 451], five centuries [of life and service by the Church], and the series of Fathers [e.g., Athanasius & Augustine] in this period—the three centuries, that is before Constantine, and the two after, determine the boundary of our Faith" (*Opuscula Posthuma*, p. 91). This great interest in the Early Church, and the desire to be reformed according to Scripture according to the way Scripture was understood and applied in the Early Church, have been often affirmed and asserted by Anglicans, at least up to recent times. Thousands have been taught in Confirmation classes: One Canon of Scripture, Two Testaments, Three Creeds, Four Ecumenical Councils, and Five Centuries of life and development, as the foundation of the Anglican Way and as that upon which the Common Prayer Tradition is based.

## THE HERITAGE REJECTED

Since the 1970s Anglican liturgists have looked back more to the second and third centuries for their inspiration and models, and they have not paid much attention to the doctrinal and liturgical developments and maturity of the fourth and fifth centuries. As a result of their work, Anglicans in the West have been experiencing a growing variety of forms of worship not only in different countries but also within countries. This has come about because of the creation and publication of a continual stream of new books and booklets of services for public worship. In the mother Church of the Anglican Family, the Church of England, this variety was made possible first by services for trial use in booklets, then the publication of *An Alternative Service Book* 1980, and most recently by *Common Worship*, in multiple volumes from 2000 onwards. In the USA, the pattern was much the same from trial services beginning in the late 1960s to the Prayer Book of 1979, followed by further booklets (e.g. *Enriching our Worship*) containing ever more varied services. There is little doubt but that these Books of varying titles have over the last thirty years begun a new tradition of public worship and prayer for Anglicanism not only in North America but also around the world. This now exists alongside the classic Common Prayer Tradition and in some ways competes with it.

In the new forms of services, the liturgists claim to be restoring valuable ancient practices and ways from the second and third centuries of the Church to modern worship, and doing so without changing basic doctrine. Yet, practically speaking, their primary thrust seems to be that of encouraging a seemingly endless variety of possibilities into divine worship and thereby introducing mediocrity into the texts and rites by the sheer volume produced at great speed. As they do so, they claim that people today want variety and choice and that they also want to address God in much the same way as they talk to one another in modern language.

Gone is one excellent form of words, and in its place are many alternatives, none of which is aesthetically memorable or theologically satisfying to the serious-minded and spiritually hungry person. Gone also in much of the new texts is the clarity of biblical and patristic teaching on fundamental matters, and in its place is often a fuzzy or simplistic presentation of basic doctrines. Further, while it is argued that this modern way involves the participation of the laity (as the people of God) in worship much more than was the case in former years, the usual position in practice is that the priest becomes the expert to choose between the variety of possible forms of service available, and then various members of the laity take part in the service of his or her choice. As was noted in the first chapter, the use of this mix-and-match liturgy is sometimes of such a character as to be guilty of the charge of dumbing-down, and this applies both to the "progressive" and the "orthodox" use of the new liturgies.

WHAT KIND OF FOUNDATION?

Of course, I am not claiming that the classic tradition of Anglican Common Prayer was or is perfect, for only the Liturgy of heaven is perfect. I am not saying that the American *BCP* (1928), Canadian *BCP* (1962), and English *BCP* (1662) would not benefit from some wise and gentle revision. It is possible that some of the new services (e.g., for Easter Eve) introduced into the recent Prayer Books could be incorporated, adapting them to the theology and ethos of the Common Prayer Tradition. Then provision could be made for the use of a revised Psalter, the kind, for example, authorized in England in 1966, and called *The Revised Psalter*, which had both C. S. Lewis and T. S. Eliot on its revision committee.

However, the major point is that the editions of *The Book of Common Prayer* of 1928, 1962, and 1662 can be improved or their contents adjusted for contemporary use, because their basic tradition is sound and well tried in all important respects. Since the foundation is solid, there is a possibility for a limited number of optional additions here and there, as long as they are done in the same style, ethos, and doctrine as the original. The grandeur and glory of the tradition of Common Prayer is that there has been a shared, excellent form of worship to be used by all who belong to a particular branch of Christendom—in this case, the Anglican Way. The excellence is not only in the choice and form of words but also in the way this tradition reflects the doctrine of Holy Scripture together with the classic, patristic, Trinitarian doctrinal and devotional heritage of the one, holy, catholic, and apostolic Church.

In contrast, the *BCP* (1979) of the USA and the *BAS* (1985) of Canada were intended, at least by some of their advocates, to create a different and opposed tradition of Christian worship. In justice, they may be called progressive or revisionist books for, where consistently used, their impact has been to destroy the received, classic tradition of Common Prayer which has been at the very center of the genius of Anglicanism from the time that the *Ecclesia Anglicana* began to use English and ceased to use Latin. In fact, this destruction is well advanced already in North America, since at least one generation—and possibly two—now exist for whom the tradition of authentic Common Prayer has not been a living, dynamic, and corporate experience or possibility.

The charge that these new collections of services and texts for liturgies (whether used as printed or further dumbed-down) are progressive and revisionist can be substantiated on various grounds, but here are four major ones.

First of all, as we have been noting, they introduce a new concept and practice of public worship. Out of the church door goes a common or shared form, content, style and language, and in the door comes a variety which is only intended to be a stage on the way to more variety. Already Liturgical Commissions have produced, and even now they continue to produce, more experimental forms of public worship, available for down-loading from web-sites or available as a loose-leaf book of possible options. In part to justify this variety, the liturgists have changed the definition of Common Prayer, which used to refer to the use by all congregations of the same basic texts for worship, expressing the beliefs held in common by the people. Now, significantly, Common Prayer has become in their way of thinking the use of services which have been authorized by a synod, have a similar or common structure and also contain certain basic common elements (e.g., the use of the Lord's Prayer & the Creed). Thus, to qualify now as Common Prayer, the content can be as varied as possible if it is placed in a specific shape and structure, has one or two common elements, and is authorized by competent authority.

In the second place, there is a definite weakening of basic Christian doctrine in the new Books. Under the cover of new liturgy, new doctrine is introduced. In fact, it is not claiming too much to say that there is evidence of a definite move to revise Christian doctrine in some places within them. One does not have to look very far with a trained eye to see that the doctrines of the Holy Trinity, of the Person and saving Work of our Lord Jesus Christ, and the nature of God's salvation for the world have all been either modified or revised. Many good and faithful Episcopalians, for example, have not noticed this doctrinal change because they have in charity assumed that the *BCP* (1979) has the same doctrine as that of the *BCP* (1928) and have read classical doctrine into the words on the pages they read, especially if they use Rite 1.

Take for example the doctrine of the Trinity. This doctrine has been preserved in the old form in the Gloria ("Glory be to the Father ... " etc.) used at the end of the Canticles and Psalms in the *BCP* (1979) as well as in the Blessing, given at the end of public worship by the bishop or priest. It has been lost, however, in other places, most obviously in the opening Acclamation or Blessing of God in Rites I and II of the Eucharist. Instead of "Blessed be God, the Father, the Son and the Holy Spirit" (for our God is One God in Three Persons), we are given a formula which is open to being read as a form of the ancient heresy of Modalism (i.e., God is One Deity and Person but has three primary Names). The new formula found all over the 1979 Book does not have the definite articles, uses a colon instead of a comma, and reads, "Blessed be God: Father, Son and Holy Spirit." Here the grammatical structure suggests that God is One Person with Three Names!

Another obvious example of change is in the use of a revised form of the Apostles' Creed. Though in the original Latin and in the long-used English translation the virginal conception of our Lord is clearly set forth in the words, "He was conceived by the Holy Spirit and born of the Virgin Mary," the revised form in Morning Prayer Rite II has the words "He was conceived by the power of the Holy Spirit and born of the Virgin Mary." The aim of the added words is to allow people who do not believe in the miraculous conception of Jesus to think of his conception as if it were like that of Isaac or John the Baptist—very special but not unique. Such an interpretation is, of course, heresy. In fact, as you survey the theological content of the *BCP* (1979), you notice a general tendency to treat and present Jesus as the Perfect Man in whom the divine presence dwells. That is, he becomes for all of us 1) a supreme example of God's presence and 2) a perfect example of human response to God in faith and love. To think in these terms of Jesus is surely something short of confessing him as "my Lord and my God."

Then serious changes are made to the translation of the Nicene Creed as that is printed in Rite II of the Eucharist (and taken from the work of the International Commission on Liturgical Texts). I urge my readers to compare the old translation "I believe … " with the new one "We believe … " in Rites I and II. There are several significant changes, and it is inappropriate to examine them all here. I simply note here the first word and state that to say "we believe" is not the same as saying "I believe." We are there together at Holy Communion as one fellowship and communion, the Body of Christ and the Bride of Christ, and as such, reckoned by heaven as a corporate person before God. The one people of God tells the Lord what it believes, confesses, and teaches on the basis of his revelation to his people, his Bride. Thus the one corporate person says "I believe." Further, each believer who is present is a member of that one Body. Each of us has to respond to the God who has revealed and given himself to us: therefore, the right response is "Lord, I believe!" Though the members of the Council of Nicea in A.D. 325 who composed the Creed said together against heretics, "We [as a body standing together] believe," they later each confessed the same Faith in Baptism and Eucharist in personal terms, "I believe" (as the text of the Creed in the ancient Orthodox Liturgies of St. Basil and St. Chrysostom shows). The modern use of "we" probably arises from the view that the church is a community of individuals (see above, chapter 1) and has to respond as such in the plural.

Thirdly, there is a definite change in the doctrine and use of the Bible. Compare, for example, the translation of Psalms 1:1 and 51:6 in the Psalter of 1928 and 1962 on the one hand and that of the same texts in 1979 and 1985 on the other. In 1:1 the original Hebrew speaks of the blessed man (male and singular): this is faithfully translated as "Blessed is the man … " by the old Psalter, the KJV, the RSV, and other versions of the Bible; but, in the American 1979 and the Canadian 1985 Psalters (which are virtually identical) we have, "happy are they … " To make matters worse, there is no note anywhere in the American 1979 Psalter to let the faithful know that they have been given a translation which is informed by the ideology of anti-sexism.

Then if you compare Psalm 51 in the old and new translations, you find that the full extent of the nature of sin is diminished in the 1979 Psalter. The human condition of sin—as inherited from others and then personally exercised—is replaced in 1979 by a notion of individual freedom of choice as exercised from one's mother's womb. Regrettably this diminution of the nature of sin harmonizes with the reduced doctrine of sin presented in the services in the rest of the Book and summarized in "The Outline of Faith or Catechism."

The Lectionary which accompanies *BCP* (1979) has certain attractive features to it, but it also has some negative aspects. There is a selective dropping of those sections of Scripture which obviously stand in definite opposition to the insights of the revised religion—this is particularly so with respect to the Letters of Paul. Where the modern mind judges him to be passing on what it chooses to call rabbinic rather than specifically Christian teaching on the relation between the male and female, or the immorality of the practice of homosexuality, then that supposed rabbinic teaching is left out (see, e.g., the omission of parts of Romans 1 and 1 Corinthians 11 & 14).

Finally, there has been revolution in the way in which God is addressed in worship. From well before the sixteenth century when English was used in private devotions, God was always addressed in the second person singular, "Thou, O Lord." In contrast, the monarch was addressed as "Your Majesty." The use of "Thou/Thee" in religious English not only did justice to the use of pronouns in the languages of the Bible, but it also, as second person singular, served two doctrinal needs—to insist that God is truly One God, and to show that he is our Father, with whom we are on intimate terms. "Thou/Thee" was the language of intimacy and thus it was somewhat bold to use this pronoun of Almighty God.

From the Renaissance of the sixteenth century through to the 1960s, English-speaking Christians read from a Bible which distinguished the second person singular from the plural ("Thou" from "You") and in worship, prayer, and hymnody addressed God only in the second person singular. The language of the King James Version and *The Book of Common Prayer* was never the street language of the sixteenth and seventeenth centuries. It was a dignified form of English which could then and can now be understood by most people with a little effort.

One effect of the change in the 1960s to a so-called contemporary, accessible English where God was addressed as "You" was to cut off a growing number of people from a rich heritage, from the tradition of worship, prayer, piety, habit, discipline, doctrine, and morality connected with the long established English language of public worship, common prayer, and private devotion. Thereby the door was opened wide to the possibility of dumbing-down.

To some people the above examples of revision of doctrine and practice may appear trivial and of little consequence. Yet to those who are familiar with the history of Christian doctrine and spirituality, they do represent important changes or deviations, which necessarily have evangelistic, ethical and pastoral repercussions.

My primary purpose is not to attack the new approach to, and ways of, worship which Episcopal and Anglican parishes are being increasingly led to experience through new provisions for public worship. Rather, it is to show that the old tradition of Common Prayer, despite its seemingly old-fashioned look, is an excellent way to know God, the living God, the God and Father of our Lord Jesus Christ, in public worship; further it is to recognize that from this knowing, trusting, and loving him comes the serving and obeying of him in daily life.

The seeking after God and the knowledge of him is the most deeply fulfilling journey upon which we can embark. We need a sure road to travel on, an accurate map to use, and a faithful guide to direct us in our search for the living God and fellowship with him. I believe that wise people will consider seriously taking that road, using that map, and employing that guide which have proved themselves over the centuries to achieve what they promise. Modern forms of transport may be better than older ones: modern houses may be warmer than older ones; but knowing God is not like using transport or buying houses. In this human quest we need to pay attention to the accumulated wisdom and tested practice of the centuries: this is more likely to lead us where we want to go than the use of untested modern insights and ways.

Of course, the old way necessarily bears traces of the historical and cultural situation in which it was first put together. Yet it has been so pruned and finely tuned over the centuries that it has achieved the position of being immediately adaptable and available to people who wish to take the call to Christian worship, prayer, and consecration seriously and are ready with sincerity and commitment to begin in earnest.

My plan for this book is governed by two major considerations. First, I want to strengthen the commitment of those who now use the *BCP* (1928, 1962, or 1662); and, secondly, I desire to encourage people who have not used a classic *BCP* to use one for the first time, if not in public, then for their personal prayer and devotion. Then, amongst my readers may be those who once used it and, being overtaken by the new ways, ceased to use it. I hope they will consider picking up where they left off and do so with enthusiasm at least in family and personal prayers.

I seek to explain first of all what is unique about knowing God and how this knowledge can truly be received and experienced only in a Liturgy where there is faithfulness to the God and Father of our Lord Jesus Christ and to his self-revelation recorded in Holy Scripture.

Having shown what it is to know God both personally and corporately, I proceed to comment on the major services and provisions of the Common Prayer Tradition in order to show how the knowing of God is presented and achieved in each (e.g., through saying and singing Daily Prayer, reading Holy Scripture, receiving Holy Communion on the Lord's Day, and participating in the Church Year).

Through this process, I attempt to show that Liturgy (the corporate worship of Almighty God through written services of worship for Baptism, Confirmation, Daily Prayer and Holy Communion) is truly the work (*ergon*) which the people (*laos*) of God do before God to glorify, magnify, and praise him. Liturgy has to do with people and work—God's believing people engaged in God's holy work, the work he has called them to offer to him. The holy work is presented before the Lord in both speech and in singing, in words and in music.

In Hebrews 8:6 the word liturgy is used of what Jesus Christ himself is now doing for his Church in heaven before the Father: "Christ has obtained a ministry [liturgy-*leitourgia*] which is as much more excellent than the old ministry [of the high priest] as the covenant he mediates is better [than the old Mosaic covenant], since it is enacted on better promises." The Church at worship is united within the new covenant to the liturgy of Christ, that is to his precious death and glorious resurrection, his ascension into heaven and his ministry there as our King, High Priest and Prophet. In the Common Prayer Tradition this union with Christ can be expected, anticipated and wonderfully achieved by the grace of God; and to this, I believe, millions in the Church Expectant and Triumphant now testify! Thanks be to God.

All in all, my aim is to show that by God's good providence there is within the Common Prayer Tradition a logic of faith, hope, and love, derived from the New Testament, and available to the flock of Christ in order that they may know God as their Father, Christ Jesus as their Shepherd and the Holy Ghost as their Counselor. This spiritual principle is intended to operate both corporately in God's people gathered as Christ's Body and in individual persons in their relation with God through Jesus Christ as his adopted children.

## MUSIC AND SINGING

Virtually all churches today make use of music and engage in singing. Looking back over the history of the Church, three different approaches to, or models of, the use of music and singing can be discerned. The first, represented by such well-known persons as Ambrose of Milan, Martin Luther of Germany, and John Wesley of England, regards music and singing as gifts of God, means of bearing God's word and enabling human beings to praise God and proclaim his Gospel. Many Episcopalians and Anglicans would hold to this model. The second, represented by Abbot Pambo of Egypt and Ulrich Zwingli of Zurich, sees little or no place for music and singing in worship, since they believed that through music and singing worldly ideas and sensuality enter the church. Few Episcopalians and Anglicans hold to this model. Finally, the third model, represented by Augustine of Hippo, Thomas Cranmer of England, and John Calvin of Geneva, admits music and singing into worship but in a limited way, seeking to control them so that they do not become an end in themselves and thus fail to serve the worship of the Holy Trinity. Not a few Episcopalians and Anglicans, especially Evangelicals, would hold to this model.

Whether it is the first or third model, or a variation of either, that is accepted by the local congregation of Christ's flock, the point is that music and singing are there to enrich and elevate what is done so that it serves its true purpose, the knowing, adoring, loving, and serving of God in worship. One the one hand, music and singing are not to be dumbed-down so that they are pedestrian and there is little in them to raise the spirit heavenward; and, on the other hand, they are not to be elevated into a show so that the service of worship is not much different from a concert. (See further the post-Vatican II document, "Instruction on Music in the Liturgy," in *Vatican Council II: The Conciliar and Post Conciliar Documents*, ed. Austin Flannery, 1981.)

TESTIMONY FROM BISHOP HENSHAW

Here is what J.P.K. Henshaw, Bishop of Rhode Island, wrote in 1831 of the excellency of *The Book of Common Prayer*:

Among the many causes of gratitude to Almighty God which distinguish our lot as Protestant Episcopalians, it is not one of the least that we are favored with a scriptural and established LITURGY; which is entitled to the warmest commendation, not only as a directory for public worship, but also as a standard and preservative of sound doctrine.

The Prayer Book has been beautifully and appropriately styled "the daughter of the Bible"; and, probably, there is no other work of human composition which has embodied so much of the substance and spirit of the heavenly Oracles. Extracts from the Bible, in the form of Gospels, Epistles and Psalter, constitute the greater part of the volume—and throughout the collects and prayers the spirit of the divine Word breathes and glows and animates the whole. What can be more chaste and spiritual than its devotional services? What more humble and meek than its penitential confessions? What more fervent and comprehensive than its acts of intercession? What more full, ardent and seraphic than its adorations and thanksgivings? How many of the followers of Christ in this day have felt their hearts glow with heavenly ardor—as if touched with a live coal from the altar—and experienced the sublime delights of spiritual communion in the use of those prayers and praises in which saints and martyrs of every age have poured forth their devotions to the Lord? And eternity only can disclose the multitude of instances in which the use of them has alleviated the pains of disease, assuaged the fears of the mariner amidst the terrors of the ocean, cheered the desolations of prison and softened the bed of death.

The LITURGY is entitled to veneration not only as a devotional work but as a compendium of sound Christian theology. All the fundamental and important doctrines of the Gospel are interwoven throughout its various offices; and while our congregations statedly use it they will he secured against the introduction of gross and flagrant heresy. (*The Communicant's Guide,* 1831, p. 3.)

The Bishop goes on to speak of the "Order for the administration of the Lord's Supper" as being nothing less than the condensing of "the excellencies of the ancient liturgies" into a wonderful English liturgy.

---

[For those who wish to pursue the criticisms I make of the 1979 Book and of modern innovations in general, I suggest that the following books will be helpful. On language and its relation to doctrine and piety see: *Neither Archaic Nor Obsolete. The Language of Common Prayer and Public Worship* by Peter Toon and Louis R. Tarsitano, 2003, Prayer Book Society of the USA & Edgeways Books, UK; on the nature and character of the Prayer Book of

1979 see: *Neither Orthodoxy Nor A Formulary. The Shape & Content of the 1979 Prayer Book*, by Louis R. Tarsitano & Peter Toon, 2004, Prayer Book Society of the USA; for a critique of the latest liturgies of the Church of England see *Common Worship Considered*, by Peter Toon, 2004, Edgeways Books, U.K. www.anglicanmarketplace.com or www.edgewaysbooks.com]

# WHAT KNOWING IS

Our subject is an exalted one—knowing God, the LORD, himself, not his creatures but knowing him, our Creator, Redeemer, Father and Judge. In what is called his high priestly prayer, Jesus prayed that they (his disciples) "might know thee, the only true God" (John 17:3). To know the heavenly Father, the God and Father of the Lord Jesus Christ, is the highest of privileges and the greatest of experiences. In order to begin to understand what such knowing is all about, it may be helpful first of all to spend a little time reflecting upon what we mean when we claim, "I know him or her," or "I know this or that thing."

## KNOWING PERSONS

To know my next-door neighbor is a more complex business than to know a place, book, language or even an animal. I can know a book or a language through learning it and know a place such as Pikes Peak in Colorado by visiting and climbing it. I can know a dog by being its owner over a period of time and exercising, feeding, training and even being dependent upon it. If it were as easy to know human persons as it is to know things and animals, the world would certainly be a different place!

There is a tendency in some of us to boast about important people with whom we have been acquainted. For example, I might, as one who was born in England, claim in a conversation, "I know Margaret Thatcher." This claim could be based on my living on the same street as she did years ago, and having had several conversations with her over the garden wall. Or you might claim that you know President Bush because you belonged to the same Rotary Club as he did twenty years ago and chatted with him at the bar.

When we speak of knowing a person, we may be referring to minimum or maximum knowledge of him or her, for there are degrees and depths of knowledge of persons. For example, I know about a lot of people through watching them on the TV screen and seeing their pictures and profiles in the newspapers and magazines. I know what they look like, how they speak, and what kinds of things they do in their career and public lives. With few, if any, of these people do I have any real personal contacts or personal relation. I merely know about aspects of their personality, career, and background. And even if what I know about them is a lot, it is still the case that I only know about them. Though I may feel I know one or two of them in a personal way, the truth of the matter is that I really and truly only know about them, for I have no meaningful personal relation with any of them.

Further, I can say much the same about most of the people I meet day by day at places where I work, enjoy leisure, and do my shopping. This also probably applies to most people in the church I attend. Certainly I may know a lot about some of them, for I may carefully observe their personality, facial expressions, words, dress, and lifestyles; but it remains true that I only know about them.

However, there are certain persons whom I really know. Not only do I know about them but I have such a personal relation with them that I actually do truly know them rather than merely knowing about them. This is possible because each of them has in different ways and by various means disclosed his or her inner life, thoughts, and being to me. Usually this personal knowing works both ways through friendship or within family ties or in holy matrimony. You reveal yourself to me and I open up myself to you—not all at once but gradually and as circumstances dictate or allow. However, it can be the case that I as a pastor am allowed confidentially to know a person because he or she has freely disclosed his or her inner life to me in order to seek my help.

WHO IS GOD?

When we speak of knowing God, we have in mind, I think, both knowing about him in terms of his nature, character, attributes, and acts and also knowing him in personal friendship. We need to know something about God, Creator, Redeemer, Father, and Judge in order to accept his gracious call to enter a personal relation of faith and trust in him and love of him. However, if we take the content of the "Ministration of Holy Baptism" seriously, then we must rejoice in the fact that God places infants in a right relation with himself from the time of their baptism. Then, within this personal relation with the Lord in the fellowship of the church, the child learns about this God in whom he trusts and grows into deepening friendship and communion with him.

As Anglicans and Episcopalians our knowledge of God is the same as that of the whole Church, Eastern and Western, Catholic and Protestant, for we all trace our history back to the same source, the apostolic Church and the Holy Scriptures. This knowledge is given the technical name of "classical Christian Trinitarian Theism" by theologians in order to distinguish it from other ways of stating a claimed knowledge of God. For example, we do not accept the ever-popular doctrine of pantheism, the doctrine that God is equivalent to nature and that the natural order is either God or the external expression of God. There have always been pantheists in western culture, poets like Walt Whitman for example. Anglicans who take their Bible and Prayer Book seriously do not believe that God is the equivalent of nature. In contrast, they confess that God is the Lord of nature.

Further, we do not accept deism, a doctrine of God popular in the eighteenth century both in America and Europe, and intimately associated with the Enlightenment. Deism is the teaching that God created the world and then left it all alone to get on with its existence. That is, like a great clockmaker, he made a clock-like universe and then wound it up to let it get on with the job of keeping time, running according to its inbuilt laws. Rejecting this approach Anglicans believe that God the Creator is also God the Sustainer and Redeemer: God cares for the world that he made *ex nihilo* (out of nothing); and by his mighty word he keeps it in existence and order moment by moment. This belief is expressed often through the use of the Psalter in the Daily Office (e.g. Ps. 29), as well as in the Canticle, *Venite*, at Morning Prayer.

So what is theism? It is the belief in one God who is the Creator of the world; he is infinite, self-existent, incorporeal, eternal, immutable, impassible, simple, omniscient, and omnipotent. These words are here used in their technical or philosophical meaning. A shorter answer is to say that God is a Spirit, infinite, eternal, and unchangeable in his being, wisdom, power, holiness, justice, goodness, and truth. A simpler way to answer the question is to say that theism is belief in one God who totally transcends (is above and wholly distinct from) the world that he made and who is perfect in wisdom, power, and love.

Historically the two chief rivals to theism have been polytheism (the belief in many gods, as in ancient Rome and Greece and in popular Hinduism today) and pantheism (the view that the world itself is divine because it is the self-expression of God's very being). Today there is also a sophisticated form of pantheism called panentheism which teaches that the self-development of God is inextricably connected with the evolution and development of the universe. This is often expressed through the process philosophy of the late A. N. Whitehead and sees God as constantly changing and growing in perfection through including within his being the experiences of the cosmos—which may he called "God's body" (as in some feminist theology).

Modern living forms of theism include Judaism and Islam. There is, of course, a profound continuity between Jewish and Christian theism for the first disciples were Jewish theists who were wholly committed to the Lord, their God. Yet, through their encounter with Jesus, as the Lord, they eventually went forth gladly to baptize converts to Christianity "in the name of the Father, the Son and the Holy Ghost." They progressed and matured in their thinking and piety from the confession of One God to the confession of One God in Trinity.

Therefore, what distinguishes classical Christian theism from any other form of theism is that Christians believe, teach, and confess that God eternally exists not only as the One and Only God but as One God in Three Persons—the Father, the Son, and the Holy Ghost. Further, Christians also hold that the eternal Son became incarnate as Jesus, the Christ, and that by him alone is there salvation from sin and into eternal life. Thus it may rightly be claimed that the "extra" beliefs concerning God, which Christians hold and Jews do not share, are based wholly on divine revelation, as that is received in and through Jesus himself and his apostles. The confession that Jesus is Lord and that Jesus is the Son of God incarnate lead on in the life of the Church to the confession that the one, eternal God is One God in Three Persons. Under the general guidance of the Holy Ghost in the Church, Christian experience of God in worship and in daily life, together with reflection upon the teaching of Jesus and the apostles against the content of the Jewish Scriptures, led to the doctrine of the Trinity. The doctrine arose to explain the vital, spiritual, and moral experience of God within the fellowship of Christians, for the Church knew and worshipped the Father through the Son in the Holy Spirit, because the Father had sent his Son into the world to be the Saviour of it.

Let us be clear. The confession of the Holy Trinity has to be stated with great care for it can be so easily misunderstood. For example, it can be carelessly stated and taken to mean that God is One God with three major names (Father, Son, and Spirit)—this was called Modalism or Sabellianism in the Early Church. Or the Trinity can be taken to mean that there are three equal Gods called the Father, the Son, and the Holy Spirit. This is tritheism. Then there is the concept of the Trinity as a descending hierarchy of three related but not equal expressions of deity. First is the Father; at a lower level of deity is the Son; and at an even lower level is the Holy Spirit. Thus only the Father is really God—the Son and the Spirit are superior angels. This is Arianism. The ancient Western Creed that we know as The Athanasian Creed or *Quicunque Vult* faces these old heresies head on.

A typical Anglican devotion for Trinity Sunday is something like this:

*Come let us adore the Sacred Trinity, Three Persons and One God.*
*To Thee, the eternal Father, made by none;*
*To Thee, the uncreated Son, begotten by the Father alone;*
*To Thee, the blessed Spirit, proceeding from the Father and the Son;*
*To Thee one, holy, consubstantial, and undivided Trinity, be as-*
    *cribed all power and wisdom and glory, now and for ever:*
*Holy holy, holy, Lord God of Sabaoth.*
*Heaven and earth are full of the Majesty of thy glory.*

The point hardly needs to be made that the constant appearance in the churches of heresies and errors in the naming and describing the Lord our God ought to make us keen to learn sound and edifying knowledge about the God whom we worship.

Here it is appropriate to mention certain modern Anglican ways of speaking of, and using, the idea of God as a Trinity, in order to provide a kind of foundation for talk of both "Christian community" and the unity and diversity of the thirty-eight Churches of the Anglican family. This modern way of describing God as "a plurality in unity" is a social doctrine of the Trinity where (a) the inner relations of the three "individualities" of the Father, Son and Holy Ghost, each different from the others, are presented as a model for "Christian community," and (b) the autonomy of each Individuality (Person) and the unity of the Three Individualities (as one God), are seen as providing a model for the diversity and unity of the Anglican Communion of Churches. Needless to say, these two uses are not to be commended for they can reduce God as Trinity merely to a human projection, created to explain and justify earthly, human arrangements. Further, they do not lead us to know God as God, but to know more of our tendency to erect idols of our own making to justify what we think and do. (See further Peter Toon, *Our Triune God*, Regent College Publishing, Vancouver, Canada.)

THE LIVING GOD

There is much to know about God, for he is like a glorious, everlastingly inexhaustible Fountain from which we drink and continue to drink. He is super-essential Being and the more we know about him the more we realize that there is more to know. Knowledge of the LORD as the Holy Trinity is fundamental, and without this knowledge we can make no progress in worship and devotion; but there are also many other aspects to the knowledge of God that we need to know in order that we might grow in our personal relation to him.

For this reason we study and meditate upon the Holy Scriptures. Anglicans have always claimed that the Scriptures of the Old and New Testament are the first source of our knowledge of God. For the Anglican who devoutly follows and uses the Lectionary in Morning and Evening Prayer there is a daily immersion in this vital source of our knowledge of the Lord our God. Further, the major aspects of the whole doctrine of God as that is provided in the Bible are woven into the wording of the various services provided in the Common Prayer tradition. For example, the teaching that God is the dynamic Creator and Sustainer of the universe and that by his providence he works all things for the purpose of his glory is clearly and reverently stated in the Collects and Prayers.

Over the centuries Christians have learned about God from being taught the Creed and the Catechism, by hearing and reading the Bible, and by accepting the teaching about God which appears in the text of the Prayer Book. This has been augmented by sermons, by further teaching, by home study groups and personal study and reflection. In the daily services of Morning and Evening Prayer there is the requirement that the participants confess their faith in the words of the Apostles' Creed—"I believe in God the Father almighty ... " In the Order for Holy Communion there is also the requirement that the Nicene or the Apostles' Creed be used. The Nicene, like the Apostles', begins in a personal way "I believe in one God ... " and goes on to state with a marvelous economy of words what I called above, classical Christian theism—Trinitarian Theism. There is yet a further official confession of faith in Anglicanism which fell into disuse from the eighteenth century onwards in America but which is, to my mind, a moving and succinct statement of the doctrine of the Trinity and the doctrine of the Person of Christ. It is the *Quicunque Vult* or the *Athanasian Creed* mentioned above: it has an integral place in the *BCP* (1662) of the Church of England and the *BCP* (1962) of Canada, but, regrettably, is not in the American edition of 1928.

In saying "I believe ... " each Christian present is speaking for himself and stating the faith of the Church. But the Church comes first for the confession is made by the Bride to the Bridegroom, by the Body to its Head, by the Household to its Master, by the congregation to its Shepherd. The individual, baptized believer, as one member of the One Body and One Household, speaks personally as he also speaks in and with the whole. It is a confession that points not only to knowledge and beliefs about God, but also to a truly personal relation with God the Father through God the

Incarnate Son. The Creed may be seen as the response of the Church and of each believer to the revelation of and salvation from God in Jesus Christ given to each of us. On the basis of what God has said and done, all together and personally we say to him, "Lord, I believe ... " Thus something of importance is lost in modern Anglican services (as noted above) where the Creed begins, "We believe ... "

This Trinitarian Theism expressed in the Nicene Creed informs the whole approach to, and content of, worship. Even though it is only stated explicitly here and there (e.g., in the *Gloria* at the end of the singing or recital of each psalm and in the final Blessing) the knowledge of God the Holy Trinity is present as the great unifying doctrine and dogma of the whole Common Prayer Tradition. Knowledge about God is intended to be the expression of personal knowing of God in the services of worship, be they the Daily Office or the Administration of the Sacraments of Baptism and Holy Communion. We are to worship the Father through and in the Son by and with the Holy Spirit. The Trinitarian structure of the services therefore exists as the vehicle for our faith-knowledge of God as Holy Trinity so that we may both pray together and as individual persons in common (i.e., genuine communal) prayer. Joined to Christ Jesus in faith and through the Holy Ghost, we join in his prayer, the prayer of the High Priest which he offers perpetually for his brethren at the right hand of the Father (Rom. 8:34). We lift up our hearts, and through the Holy Ghost we are united to him as our Mediator. He is the Head and we are the members of his Body. and therefore being in him we are united by grace to the Holy Trinity for eternal life.

> *Almighty and everlasting God, who hast given unto us thy servants grace, by the confession of a true faith, to acknowledge the glory of the eternal Trinity, and in the power of the Divine Majesty to worship the Unity: We beseech thee, that thou wouldest keep us steadfast in this faith, and evermore defend us from all adversities, who livest and reignest one God, world without end. Amen.*

In the words of the *Quicunque Vult*: "the Catholic Faith is this: That we worship one God in Trinity, and Trinity in Unity." And thus we often sing or say: "Glory be to the Father, and to the Son and to the Holy Ghost: as it was in the beginning, is now and ever shall be, world without end. Amen."

Addressing God in corporate worship and prayer has always been a godly exercise offered both in speaking and singing. Throughout the Bible there are many references to singing unto, and singing before, the Lord our

God. In the New Testament singing is guided and empowered by the Holy Ghost and is the expression of conscious faith, hope and love. There is no making music for its own sake but rather for expressing the word of God in and through it. In prison Paul and Silas spent the hours of the night praying and singing hymns unto God (Acts 16:25). Then Paul told the Christians in Ephesus: "Be filled with the Spirit, addressing one another in psalms and hymns and spiritual songs, singing and making melody to the Lord with all your heart" (5:18–19). To the Christians in Colosse he had similar advice: "Let the word of God dwell in you richly, teach and admonish one another in all wisdom, and sing psalms and hymns and spiritual songs with all thankfulness in your hearts to God" (3:16).

Then, in the last book of the Bible, we encounter perfect congregational singing, as the angel choirs, joined by redeemed humanity, never cease to sing the praise of God: "Holy, holy, holy, is the Lord God Almighty, who was, and is, and is to come!" (Revelation 4:8; see also 4:11; 5:9–10; 11:17–18; 15:3–4; 16:4–7; 19:6–8). What is good for heaven is surely good for earth, and what is good for the Church triumphant is also good for the Church militant here on earth. The one, holy, catholic and apostolic Church must sing unto and before the Lord her God; she can do no other, for he is utterly and completely praiseworthy and adorable. In the Anglican Way, as in the Roman Catholic and Orthodox Ways, there is, therefore, provision for addressing the Holy Trinity in speech and in song, as we shall notice when we look at both the Daily Service and the Service of Holy Communion.

WISDOM FROM BISHOP HOBART

In his *Companion to the Festivals and Fasts* (1804) Bishop John Henry Hobart of New York had the following explanations of Common Prayer.

*Q. Since our Church has prescribed a form of prayer or Liturgy, for the public service of the Church, state some of the particular advantages of forms of prayer.*

A. When a form of prayer is used, the people are previously acquainted with the prayers in which they are to join, and are thus enabled to render unto God a reasonable and enlightened service. In forms of prayer, the greatest dignity and propriety of sentiment may be secured. They prevent the particular opinions and dispositions of the minister from influencing the devotions of the congregation; they serve as a standard of faith and practice; and they render the service more animating, by uniting the people with the minister in the performance of public worship.

Q. *What are the peculiar excellences of the Liturgy prescribed by our Church?*

A. In the Liturgy of our Church there is an admirable mixture of instruction and devotion. The Lessons, the Creeds, the Commandments, the Epistles and Gospels, contain the most important and impressive instruction on the doctrines and duties of religion; while the Confession, the Collects and Prayers, the Litany and Thanksgivings, lead the understanding and the heart through all the sublime and affecting exercises of devotion. In this truly evangelical and excellent Liturgy, the supreme Lord of the universe is invoked by the most appropriate, affecting and sublime epithets; all the wants to which man, as a dependent and sinful being, is subject, are expressed in language at once simple, concise, and comprehensive; these wants are urged by confessions the most humble, and supplications the most reverential and ardent; the all-sufficient merits of Jesus Christ, the Saviour of the world, are uniformly urged as the only effectual plea, the only certain pledge of divine mercy and grace; and with the most instructive lessons from the sacred oracles, and the most profound confessions and supplications, is mingled the sublime chorus of praise, begun by the minister, and responded with one heart and voice from the assembled congregation.

The mind, continually passing from one exercise of worship to another, and, instead of one continued and uniform prayer, sending up its wishes and aspirations in short and varied collects and supplications, is never suffered to grow languid or weary. The affections of the worshipper ever kept alive by the tender and animating fervor which breathes through the service, he worships his God and Redeemer in spirit and in truth, with reverence and awe, with lively gratitude and love; the exalted joys of devotion are poured upon his soul; he feels that it is good for him to draw near unto God, and that a day spent in his courts is better than a thousand passed in the tents of the ungodly.

# COVENANT WITH GOD

W[e need to take time now to reflect upon the nature of the relation which we have by grace with God, since the way we understand this will determine to a large measure our attitudes within common prayer and worship. If I come to common worship thinking that my relation with God is that of an equal or near-equal partner with him then my attitude will reflect that mindset. If I come thinking that I am doing God some kind of favor or showing him some special loyalty, then my attitude will reflect this mindset. In contrast, if I come in gratitude and humility, conscious of my sins and unworthiness but overwhelmed by God's mercy to me in Jesus Christ, then my mindset and attitude will be what they ought to be in the presence of the merciful and holy Lord.

## GOD'S INITIATIVE

In the Bible God enters into a relation with believing sinners and their children through what is called his covenant of grace. We tend to think of a covenant as an agreement or contract between two parties who are of the same kind or who are equal in some way or another. The Old Testament contains references to such covenants—e.g., agreements between kings. However, God's covenant with man is not an agreement between equals, and it is not a contract to which both sides agree. It is a totally one-sided affair because God alone establishes it and in doing so he sets out its terms and conditions. Then to remind us of our sinful, creaturely status and reduce our pride, God tells us that we can fulfill the conditions of the covenant as his covenant partners only with his help. In fact, without the help of the Holy Ghost we cannot even enter, let alone live rightly within, God's covenant of grace as his children.

On first consideration, this may seem to be dictatorial and tyrannical action by God. Yet, if we take time to reflect upon such a covenant, we shall see that we are not talking of two equal partners but of the Lord God, the Creator and Sustainer of the universe, whom the angels serve and adore and who is infinitely above our being and our thought. He is God and we are mere creatures—finite and sinful, spiritually and morally diseased creatures! Further, if we recognize that his covenant is truly a covenant of grace and is established for our good and eternal welfare, that we may become his children and be restored to genuine knowing and loving of him for all eternity, then we shall probably admit not only that he has every right to act as he has, but also that he has acted in mercy and compassion towards us by establishing his covenant of grace with us and for us in Christ Jesus. For the simple fact is that we of ourselves cannot help ourselves in terms of lifting ourselves up to God in order to negotiate with him. He must come down and towards us. His covenant of grace is his coming towards us so that we can draw near to him.

The initiative and grace of God in our salvation is most clearly understood and presented in the *BCP* (1928), as in *BCP* (1962). The First Office of Instruction of the Catechism in *BCP* (1928) begins with this Collect, which is also that for the seventh Sunday after Trinity:

> *Lord of all power and might, who art the author and giver of all good things; graft in our hearts the love of thy name, increase in us true religion, nourish us with all goodness, and of thy great mercy keep us in the same; through Jesus Christ our Lord. Amen.*

Its words clearly point both to the initiative of God towards us and of his help to us in fulfilling our duties within his covenant. He is the "author" and "giver," and it is he alone who can "increase", "nourish," and "keep" his believing children in his grace and covenant. Our genuine freedom is not to assert our sinful selves. Rather, it is to be free from sin, its guilt and power, and to do his bidding with his gracious help.

In contrast the *BCP* (1979) does not have this clarity of commitment to the initiative and assistance of God in his relations with his people. Lurking there both in its Catechism ("An Outline of the Faith") and in some of the Collects (e.g. that of the First Sunday after the Epiphany, which refers to the covenant as being made by those who are baptized!) is the tendency to treat human beings as if they were negotiating, near-equal covenant partners with God! This tendency reflects, of course, the pride of modern man, who refuses to recognize that he is not merely in rebellion against God (which *BCP* 1979 certainly seems to teach) but, also, that he is so sick and diseased by sin that he cannot truly help himself (which *BCP* 1979 appears to downplay or reject). For the Bible and the classic *BCP* "there is no health in us" and so we need to see the Divine Physician!

THE BIBLICAL TEACHING

God's relation with human beings is established and begins with his role of the Creator of the created. This relation can never change, for, however ennobled man becomes, he can never rise to be like God. He will always be a finite, dependent, and contingent being looking unto God in whom, as Paul declares, he lives and moves and has his being (Acts 17:28). However, within this relation, which man has marred by sinfulness and rebellion, God has moved to establish a further relation of grace and unmerited favor, whose full content is a new creation.

The Lord God began this new relation when he declared, "I will establish my covenant" (Gen. 6:18; Ex. 6:4–5). Then the essence of the covenant was captured by God's declaration: "I will take you to me for a people and I will be to you a God" (Ex. 6:7; see also Gen. 17:7 & Rev. 21:2–3). The covenant is unilateral in origin and establishment: it is not only offered, but it is given unto Abraham and his descendants, who receive it but cannot negotiate its nature or content. However, the covenant of grace is two-sided when it comes into practical effect in human lives, for the recipients, first Israel and then the Church, become by God's mercy and choice his covenant partners. He is to them their LORD, and they are to worship, trust, love, and obey him as he directs (Deut. 7:9, 13; 1 Kings 8:23).

God established his covenant of grace with Abraham (Gen. 17:7) and his descendants. On Mount Sinai a special administration of this covenant was established with Israel through Moses (see Ex. 19ff.). In the Five Books of Moses (Genesis to Deuteronomy) we learn not only of what God's initiative and relation meant, but also what were the covenant obligations of the people of Israel. While God promised to be the living God who would guide, protect, bless, and care for them as his elect people, they in turn were committed to be his people on his terms and according to his conditions. In their relation to him there were no negotiating possibilities, for he was their God, who had brought them up out of the land of Egypt and who would lead them into the promised land. The Ten Commandments began with a statement of faith—the God who commands is the living God who has redeemed and will guide his people (see Ex. 20:1–2).

In the rest of the Old Testament (= Old Covenant) we read both of God's continuing faithfulness to his elect people and of their imperfect response to his gracious mercy and guidance. The story of the Books of Samuel, Kings, and Chronicles is the story more of failure to be his faithful covenant partners than of success in that vocation. Much of what the prophets declared was a word from heaven calling upon the Israelites to fulfill their covenantal duties. The people were called to know their Lord God and in knowing him to reject other gods; but so often they chose not to know him and to go after Baal and the gods of Canaan. Yet, despite their apostasy and pride, God, the LORD, remained their covenant God, never forgetting them.

Worship without Dumbing-down ◆ 37

Speaking through Jeremiah the Lord God addressed his covenant people in these words:

> Let not the wise man glory in his wisdom, neither let the mighty man glory in his might, let not the rich man glory in his riches; but let him that glorieth glory in this, that he understandeth and knoweth me, that I am the LORD which exercise lovingkindness, judgment, and righteousness in the earth; for in these I delight (9:23–24).

The LORD delights to see in his creatures a true knowledge of himself. Through Hosea he said: "For I desired mercy and not sacrifice; and the knowledge of God more than burnt offerings" (6:6). Within the Mosaic covenant what God looked for in and through the use of the Temple, the sacrificial system and priesthood, and the administration of the Law was a people who knew him and thus worshipped and served him from within revealed knowledge.

With the Incarnation of the eternally begotten Son of God, the Word made flesh, God revealed the length and breadth, height and depth, of his mercy and of his covenant of grace. In and through Jesus Christ, God the Father established what Jesus himself called "a new covenant" (see Matt. 26:26–30)—the fullness of his covenant of grace. In the atoning, reconciling work of Jesus, God made possible for people of all races at all times and in all places what he had offered and given to Israel in a limited space and time. By his sacrificial death and shed blood Jesus established the covenant of grace on new foundations. He became the Mediator through whom believing sinners come to God for the cleansing of their sins, the gift of eternal life, and the privilege to call him "Father."

Jesus Christ is now the Way, the Truth and the Life, and no one comes to the Father except through him. And those who come in faith to the Father in and through him are not only adopted as the children of God, but God also desires to dwell in their souls as he promised through Jeremiah, the prophet. "Behold ... I will make a new covenant ... I will put my law in their inward parts and write it in their hearts; and I will be their God and they shall be my people ... They shall all know me from the least of them unto the greatest of them" (31:31–34). This is not merely knowing about God; it is knowing God, through direct communion with him in corporate and personal prayer and trusting relation.

Anyone who carefully reads the New Testament (the account of how the new covenant was established by God the Father through God the Son by God the Holy Spirit) must see and understand that the relation with God through faith and by the agency of the Holy Ghost is genuinely personal and dynamic. It is a relation which operates in both directions from God to man and from man to God. The human movement to the Father through Jesus Christ is always dependent upon his primary movement through Jesus Christ and in the Holy Ghost to his children. Within this covenant God calls his people into ever deepening fellowship, union, and communion with himself, for he delights to be known by his redeemed creatures. Has he not made them in order that they might enjoy and love him forever? Human knowing of God begins in personal and corporate prayer, but it is extended from prayer into the whole of life, for God calls his people to walk with him and to be aware everywhere and at all times of his presence with them. Paul himself wrote of knowing God in his sufferings with and for Christ as he proclaimed the Gospel in the Roman Empire (see e.g. 2 Cor. 4-6).

In his marvelous Letter to the Romans, Paul made much use of the word "justification," a word closely tied to "righteousness" and "justice." He used it to explain what it means to be in a covenant relation with God through believing the Gospel (see Rom. 1:16–17; 3:21–31 & 5:1–2). It is to be placed by God himself in a right relation with God because of the merits of Jesus Christ, through whom our sins are forgiven and the way to communion with God restored. It is to be declared and accounted righteous or just (in God's heavenly court) and to be placed in the way of becoming righteous and just. To be justified by faith is to be in God's covenant of grace and to be the recipient of his covenant mercy and faithfulness. It is to know him as God, for he has placed believers in a right relation with himself. Previously in their sinfulness they were in a wrong or non-relation; but now by grace they are in the most intimately close relation possible with him, for they are heirs and joint-heirs with Christ of the kingdom of God (Rom.8:17). In fact Paul makes it clear in his Letters that we only know God because he first knew us (see 1 Cor. 8:3; 13:12 & Gal. 4:9). God entered into personal contact with sinful human beings through the Incarnate Son and by the Holy Ghost. Only on this basis of his knowing them can they know him.

To be placed in the way of personal, practical righteousness, which is the inner life of the new covenant, means being united with Jesus Christ in faith and by the Holy Ghost. Thus in Romans 8 Paul describes the intimacy which God, the Father, establishes with his adopted children. He places in their hearts the Holy Ghost whom he names the Spirit of Christ. By his presence believers are enabled to cry out from the depths of their beings "Abba" (the familiar name for father in the Jewish home). Further, they experience the Spirit himself praying through them, uttering prayers they themselves could never compose. Their spiritual prayer and their consecrated life is a response to the heavenly Father's gracious, loving initiative and continuing faithfulness. The response of believers becomes a life of maturity in faith, hope, and love.

There is a broad range of images used in the New Testament to show the relation of God to those who are united to the Lord Jesus Christ in faith. We may recognize their personal nature by briefly noticing four. 1) God is the heavenly Father and believers are his adopted children, the brethren of Christ and joint-heirs with him of the Father's kingdom. Thus we pray, "Our Father." Further, 2) God (or Jesus Christ as the God-Man) is the Lord and King, and believers are his subjects and servants, who live to render him humble service. Then 3) God (or Jesus Christ as the God-Man) is the Shepherd and believers are his sheep. Jesus said, "I am the good shepherd and know my sheep … my sheep hear my voice and I know them" (John 10:14*ff.*).

God (or Jesus Christ as the God-Man) is 4) the Bridegroom who loves the Church; and in response the Church is the Bride who likewise loves and obeys the Bridegroom. This image from holy matrimony points to a vital intimacy, and it is interesting to observe that the Hebrew verb "to know" can and does refer sometimes in the Old Testament to the intimate act of sexual intercourse (e.g., 1 Sam. 1:19, "Elkanah knew Hannah, his wife"). Therefore the knowing of the Bridegroom (Jesus) by the Bride (the Church) points to deep spiritual union and communion of the members with Christ himself and because with him, therefore also with the Father, and with one another "in Christ."

GOD AND SELF

Archbishop Cranmer and those who assisted him in the composition of the first two editions of *The Book of Common Prayer* in the sixteenth century were greatly influenced by the Letter to the Romans. Traces of its teaching can be found at many points, not least in the service of Holy Communion. Another theme which is found in Common Prayer is the ancient Christian wisdom that all Christian holiness is contained in two things—the knowledge of God and the knowledge of self. Often Augustine of Hippo, whose *Confessions* is a true classic and whose writings have always been prized by Anglicans, exclaimed, "Lord, that I may know thee and that I may know myself!" To claim that this prayer is a summary of the Common Prayer tradition of piety and devotion would not be an excessive claim! I think it is generally true.

The knowledge of God elevates the Christian believer while right knowledge of self keeps him humble. Knowing God may be said to be that ascent wherein the congregation of Christ's flock contemplates the divine perfections and glory, while knowing self may be said to be that descent which makes God's people see their own weakness and sinfulness. That knowledge of God which raises the believer up to God also simultaneously humbles him by the comparison of himself with God, as he is revealed in Jesus. Further, genuine self-knowledge, though it humbles the believer, also lifts him up through the necessity of approaching God to find comfort, forgiveness, and solace through Christ Jesus. The true elevation of the people of God is inseparable from true humiliation—which is made crystal clear in the Anglican Common Prayer Tradition. To elevate man without humbling him is to cause pride; and to humble him without exalting him is to bring misery without hope. Thus to complain, as do some modern teachers of liturgy, that the Common Prayer Tradition is preoccupied with concerns of guilt, sin, and justification is to go against the wisdom of Scripture and Christian tradition. Unless worshippers see their sin, guilt, and hopelessness, how can they see that in Jesus Christ alone is their salvation?

To know self is as necessary for holiness as to know God. To know self is to treat the self justly, for to know ourselves as we really are is to see ourselves as God himself sees us. Consider the question, Who am I? In and of myself I am as nothing, for from all eternity I was not, and there was no reason in my own being as to why I should exist or be who or what I am. My existence is the effect of God's will alone—not mine or anyone else's. Were God to withdraw his powerful, sustaining word and power, my being would cease to be. All I am and can be comes from God and is dependent upon him, and thus there is nothing in myself to love. In fact, since I have sinned against my Creator, I justly deserve his punishment. I have offended and continue to offend the Lord my God. I have become his enemy, and I transgress his law. I fail in essential duties to him and my fellow creatures, for in me the tendency to sin has become a fixed habit and a strong inclination. Further, I cannot help myself out of this mess. God himself must lift me up if I am to be raised.

A significant statement is left out of the General Confession in Morning Prayer in Rite I of *BCP* (1979). On first sight the Confession from *BCP*

(1928) and (1979) appear to be the same but the reality of original sin or the diseased, deceitful heart (Jer. 17:9; Mark 7:18–23) is missing from the latter. As noted above, the statement, "There is no health in us," is profoundly true, and this is wholly recognized by those, tutored by Holy Scripture, who see themselves as God sees and knows them.

Thus we learn from our Bibles and Prayer Books that to be genuine Christians we must recognize and admit that we are nothing of ourselves, that we receive all things from God, both in the order of nature and of grace; and, further, that we expect all things from him in the order of glory in the age to come. As the Collect for the Fourth Sunday after Trinity puts it:

> O God, the protector of all that trust in thee, without whom nothing is strong, nothing is holy; Increase and multiply upon us thy mercy; that, thou being our ruler and guide, we may so pass through things temporal, that we finally lose not the things eternal. Grant this, O heavenly Father, for the sake of Jesus Christ our Lord. Amen.

This knowing of God and self, inspired by the Holy Ghost, is in part intellectual, but it also is a knowing by the heart. By this knowledge of God the whole soul is penetrated, reformed, renewed, and ennobled so that it begins to want to know and to love what God himself commands and loves. To know God is to possess a lively faith, a firm hope, an ardent love, a filial fear and reverence, a total trust in him in times of trial and testing, and an entire submission to his gracious and perfect will. This is the form of knowing taught and encouraged by the Common Prayer Tradition, but, at best, present only in minimal form in the new types of public prayer used by Episcopalians and Anglicans.

To know God is thus a knowing by the whole soul. It is to know God in and through the mind (to have right thoughts about him and to contemplate him through his self-unveiling in Revelation), in and through the heart (to direct one's affections to him so as to trust him and his Word, to delight in him, love him, rejoice in his grace, and fear his holy name) and through the will (in the obedience of faith in daily life). Of course, people are different for some are more intellectual than others, while some are more affective than others. For some the mind descends into the heart in knowing God while for others the heart rises to contain the mind in knowing God. There is certainly place for both types of personalities, and the Common Prayer Tradition is wide enough for all kinds of people who come to the knowledge of God in faith and by love in different ways. What this tradition does not cater to is merely an affective knowing—that is, a religion only of feelings. Instruction in basic Christian doctrine and biblical teaching is fundamental to the Anglican Way, and this intellectual understanding ought to be there even in people who are primarily affective or feeling persons.

## HIS MAJESTY

One of the great losses in modern worship, and thus in modern Christianity, is that of the inner sense and profound appreciation of the glorious Majesty, the wonderful transcendence and greatness of the Lord our God. "The Lord reigneth, he is clothed with majesty" (Ps. 93:1); "I will speak of the glorious honor of thy majesty" (Ps. 145:5). This recognition of Majesty has been called "a sense of the numinous" and "the fear of the Lord." So often Anglicans have sung: "The LORD is a great God and a great King ... O come let us worship and bow down" (Ps. 95). In the Bible one of the most obvious examples of the recognition of Majesty is the abasement and attitude of Isaiah in the Temple when he saw the glorious majesty of God, the King above all kings, and heard the angelic cry of worship, "Holy, Holy, Holy" (Is. 6). This cry is repeated in the liturgy of heaven as recorded in the Book of Revelation (4:8) and it became a central element in the liturgy of the Catholic Church in the Eucharistic Prayer.

Where this deep conviction and inner sense of the transcendent, awesome Mystery (*Mysterium Tremendum*) who is God, is absent from the Church, there is not only a loss in the quality of worship, but also the beginnings of practical errors and evils within the churches. Today, so few apparently seem to be aware of this loss of the sense of "his Majesty" because any vital sense of divine transcendence is both absent from the surrounding culture and from the popular religious mind in the West.

Few Christians and even fewer priests and preachers appear to have high and lofty thoughts of the LORD our God: instead of being lost in wonder, love, and praise at the thought of his Majesty, we tend to think of him only as around us and with us here and now. Of course God is omnipresent in the created order by his Spirit and thus immanent in this world; but he is immanent only because he is first transcendent, high and lifted up as Isaiah saw and knew him in his vision. Perhaps the problem is that we think from the immanence of God towards his transcendence rather than the biblical way of from his transcendence to his immanence. In fact, it is probably true that there is an emerging sense of the irrelevance of the older Christian doctrine of the transcendence of the Lord our God in many churches, since modern people appear to need a God with whom they can easily identify, be a part of, and negotiate with, as with a Friend who is close by.

If we could regain the conviction in mind and heart that it is only by the creating and sustaining dynamic word of the LORD that each of us and everything around us actually exists and is kept in being, then we would possibly realize that God, the Creator, must be transcendent to be immanent. He is the transcendent Creator, the infinite, eternal Majesty on high, glorious in holiness and perfect in purity, wholly beyond our thoughts and aspirations. After recognizing that, we would also begin to appreciate both his mercy and grace in revealing himself to us, and also his infinite condescension in becoming Man, bone of our bone and flesh of our flesh. To this end we could do nothing more useful than meditate upon Isaiah 40:12*ff.* where the greatness and majesty of God is so very powerfully presented: "To whom will ye compare me that I should be like him? says the Holy One" (verse 25).

We learn in the Book of Proverbs, that the fear of the Lord is not only the beginning of wisdom but also the beginning of knowledge. There can be godly fear in the soul only when there are large views of God and small views of man. Filial fear is not fear of being judged and cast into hell, but it is the awe, reverence, humble trust, and profound sense of dependence of the child of God upon the holy Lord God of hosts. This godly fear is encouraged in the Common Prayer Tradition by the repeated addressing of God as "Almighty God" at the beginning of Collects.

The Lord our God is holy with an absolute, almighty holiness that knows no degrees; and this he cannot impart to his creatures for he is God, and they are the loving work of his creative power. Yet there is a relative and contingent holiness which the Lord shares with the holy angels in heaven and with believing sinners on earth. The will of God is the sanctification of mankind in Christ, and his command in both the Old and New Testaments is, "Be ye holy for I am holy" (Lev. 11:44; 1 Pet. 1:16). God shares his holiness with those who know him through the imputation of Christ's righteousness (in Justification) and impartation of the indwelling Holy Ghost (in Sanctification). The Common Prayer Tradition faithfully sets forth this sharing, especially in the Order for Holy Communion—"that he may dwell in us and we in him."

Knowing God as his adopted child begins for the Christian at Holy Baptism by spiritual regeneration. In the case of adults, there will have been a preliminary and preparatory knowing as they are drawn to Christ in what we may call an initial conversion and as they begin to prepare for full incorporation into Christ, crucified and risen, and membership of his Body, the Church.

In the third and fourth centuries of the Christian era, adults went through a long period of preparation in the catechetical schools before the final preparation in Lent leading to baptism on Easter Eve. In modern times we have generally made the preparation less exacting, but there are moves afoot to recover a longer and deeper preparation for entry into the full fellowship of the church. Such preparation is so necessary today for the tentacles of secular culture have entered our minds and hearts and corrupted them. The corruption has been so thorough that we need a reconstructed view of God and of the world in order to develop Christian thinking, feeling, and acting, and to have a genuine Christian mindset. One problem is: Do we have the clergy and lay leadership to do this teaching?

With infants there is no obvious preliminary knowing of God, and thus their knowing of God—or more strictly God's gracious knowing them as his adopted children—begins at Baptism and comes to fruition with Confirmation. At least this is how it ought to be in right conditions; but, in this instance God's grace coming to fruition in their lives is in part dependent upon faithful nurturing and teaching of the baptized children by parents and godparents (sponsors). Observation suggests that the actual coming to know God in a personal way occurs more readily and easily when the baptized infant is surrounded by faithful prayer, godly example, and sound teaching.

Originally what we call Baptism and Confirmation belonged together and were one, occurring in the one service and often at Easter Eve in the early centuries of the Church. However, from the fifth century onwards, and with the great increase in the number of people professing Christianity, many more infants than adults were brought for Baptism. Thus the separation of Confirmation (really in origins the last part of the rite of baptism) from Baptism developed in the West (but not in the East, where the priest administered chrism [anointing with oil] as part of the Baptism of infants).

So it is not altogether surprising that in the West, from the early Middle Ages to the modern day, the precise relation of Baptism and Confirmation has sometimes not been as clearly stated as it could have been: and this is reflected in such questions as whether Confirmation should be treated as a Sacrament in its own right, and whether or not baptized children should be brought to, or encouraged to, receive Holy Communion before their Confirmation. (Part of the confusion in the Episcopal Church has been caused by the claim in *BCP* (1979) that "initiation is complete in Baptism," that giving Communion to infants is proper and that Confirmation is in no way a Sacrament. This reflects a modern ecumenical approach and is an innovation in the historic Anglican Way.)

BAPTISM

There is provision both for the baptism of adults and infants in the *BCP* (1928). The rite and Sacrament of holy Baptism has five parts to it: (1) the Preparation (which represents what has survived from the ancient catechetical ceremonies of the early Church); (2) the promises of the candidates or their sponsors/godparents taking on the duties of the covenant of grace; (3) the Blessing of the water in the Font; (4) the act of Baptism, and (5) a final Thanksgiving.

In the first part consisting of an exhortation, prayers, and reading of the Gospel, the truth that it is God who calls and brings people into covenant with himself and thus into his Kingdom and Church is most clearly acknowledged. In fact this understanding is summarized in the prayer: "*Almighty and everlasting God, heavenly Father, we give thee humble thanks that thou hast vouchsafed to call us to the knowledge of thy grace and faith in thee: increase this knowledge and confirm this faith in us evermore. Give thy Holy Spirit to this child (this thy servant), that he may be born again, and be made an heir of everlasting salvation....*" Also in this introductory section the theological meaning of Baptism is made clear, based on the word of Jesus in John 3. Baptism is a spiritual birth, a birth from above by the operation of the Holy Ghost, whereby the believer or infant receives an earnest of the inheritance in the eternal kingdom of God and also is made a member of the Body of Christ, the Church of God. While the outward and visible sign is water, the inward and spiritual grace given by God causes a death unto sin and a new birth unto righteousness and to adoption as God's child.

The promises made by the one to be baptized or the sponsors of the infant may be described as the response to the grace of God offered to mankind in general and to each person in particular in Jesus Christ. A human being can promise to turn from sin, evil, and the Devil to serve the Lord only because

God has come to him, called him, and promised him the riches of his grace. It is important to note that he says, "I will, by God's help," and that human promises are immediately followed by four supplications which, in addressing the God of all mercy for help, give expression to the mystical, spiritual, and moral meaning of baptism. For example, the first supplication is:

*O merciful God, grant that like as Christ died and rose again, so this child [or this thy servant] may die to sin and rise to newness of life.*

The Blessing of the Font is an ancient practice since prayers for the sanctification of the water formed a part of the baptismal liturgy from earliest times. The physical water does not change its chemical composition through prayer; but, it is consecrated or set aside to be the outward and visible expression of an inward and spiritual cleansing. In fact it is related in its spiritual function to the water and blood which flowed from our Lord's pierced side (John 19:34), which point to his own Baptism in water and later in blood. The last part of the Prayer/Blessing requests God our Father "to grant [out of his bounty] that this child ... may receive the fullness of thy grace, and ever remain in the number of thy faithful children ... " Once again therefore, we see that the prerogative is with God; human beings are the recipients, not the initiators, of grace. All that they have is from God and by God in grace.

The formula of Baptism is taken from Matthew 28:19 and is a fully Trinitarian formula. To pronounce the threefold Name of the Three Persons of the One God over a person is to state and confess that he or she belongs to God and is his forever. The Name of God here stands for God as God, God himself, and thus we hallow the name of God. In other words, God is admitting this person into full membership of his covenant of grace. To sign him, or her, with the sign of the Cross makes clear that the covenant of grace is intimately centered on Jesus Christ, who was crucified: thus those who are in Christ are to take up their cross, follow him, and continue in his name the war against the world, the flesh, and the devil, until he comes again in power and glory.

Finally, grateful hearts offer Thanksgiving for the union of the baptized with the Lord Jesus Christ, who was crucified and died but who is risen from the dead and reigns in glory. They have died to sin and are alive to God in Christ Jesus and must now put this divine truth into practical daily living with the ever-present help of the Holy Ghost. With infants the initial responsibility to make the presence of Christ effective in their lives devolves of course upon the godliness of parents and sponsors.

There is a solemn duty laid upon the local church to pray for those who have been baptized as infants and await their Confirmation. In *BCP* (1928) a Collect for children encourages this constant prayer:

> *O Lord Jesus Christ, who dost embrace children with the arms of thy mercy, and dost make them living members of thy Church; give them grace, we pray thee, to stand fast in thy faith, to obey thy word and to abide in thy love; that, being made strong by the Holy Spirit, they may resist temptation and overcome evil, and may rejoice in the life that now is, and dwell with thee in the life that is to come; through thy merits O merciful Saviour, who with the Father and the Holy Ghost livest and reignest one God, world without end. Amen.*

To pray thus is to encourage parents and sponsors in the privilege and duty of bringing children up in "the nurture and admonition of the Lord."

The substance of the teaching to be given to baptized children before they are brought to Confirmation is given in the Catechism or Offices of Instruction. As the covenant partners of God they are to know what his law is (the Ten Commandments), what the Faith is (the Apostles' Creed), and how to pray (the Lord's Prayer). Further, they are to know what are the sacraments of the new covenant and who are the ministers of Christ in the Church. The Collects which are included in the Offices make it abundantly clear that it is possible to please God only through the assistance of his grace. For example:

> *O Almighty God, who alone canst order the unruly wills and affections of sinful men; grant unto thy people, that they may love the thing which thou commandest, and desire that which thou dost promise; that so, among the sundry and manifold changes of the world, our hearts may surely there be fixed, where true joys are to be found; through Jesus Christ our Lord. Amen.*

Another Collect asks that the baptized may have "the spirit to think and do always such things as are right," for in and of ourselves we cannot do any good [i.e., good that is good before God himself].

I often think of a Latin expression used by Martin Luther. Each morning as he arose from his bed he would say aloud, "*Baptizatus sum*" (I have been baptized; that is, I am a baptized Christian). In saying this he was reminding himself of what it means to be baptized (and confirmed) and he was expressing his prayer that each day he would live as one who in Christ has died to sin and who in Christ is to be filled with the new, resurrection life of Christ, which is the life of the kingdom of God. There is a very intimate connection between the state of being baptized and the vocation to live a genuinely Christian life. Although all is of grace, there is a real sense also in which all is of the baptized believer. This truth is captured in the stanza:

> I would not work my soul to save
> For that my Lord has done.
> But I would work like any slave,
> For love of God's dear Son.

I believe we can learn and profit from what Luther said and practiced, for we all are called to demonstrate in daily living the meaning of our baptism into Christ. And, as Confirmation makes clear, we can do so because, and only because, of the presence and power of the Holy Ghost, who indwells the souls of the baptized.

## CONFIRMATION

Confirmation is intimately related to Baptism and is rightly thought of as the conclusion of the sacrament of Holy Baptism. It may be called a sacrament in the sense that it is the final part of the rite of Baptism, which has been held back until such time as the child truly understands and appreciates what is the content of the covenantal obligation to God, that already by grace he or she stands in. Thus as long as the Church advocates and practices infant baptism, so long ought she to take Confirmation seriously. And First Communion should normally follow Confirmation.

Confirmation is necessary to provide the opportunity for the fulfilling of the aspects of the human side of the covenant of grace (i.e., public commitment to Jesus Christ as Lord). Further, from a practical point of view, it is most useful as the opportunity to provide sound, preparatory instruction to those who are now seriously taking on the duties of the baptismal commitments (already promised on their behalf by their sponsors). Here preparation for Confirmation functions in much the same way as did preparation for Baptism in the Early Church and as catechetical teaching functions in missionary situations today.

Where the local church is truly concerned for the spiritual and moral welfare of those to be confirmed, she prays for them. A Collect is actually provided in BCP (1928) for this obligation:

> O God, who through the teaching of thy Son Jesus Christ
> didst prepare the disciples for the coming of the Comforter;

*make ready, we beseech thee, the hearts and minds of thy
servants who at this time are seeking to be strengthened by
the gift of the Holy Spirit through the laying on of hands,
that, drawing near with penitent and faithful hearts, they
may evermore be filled with the power of his divine indwelling; through the same Jesus Christ our Lord. Amen.*

The making ready is both a work of God and a work of man. God does his work invisibly through the ministry of the Holy Spirit, but the local church does her work through wise teaching, judicious pastoral care, and fervent praying for those to be confirmed.

Now to the service itself, which is simple and brief. Those to be confirmed are presented to the bishop, who asks them whether they are ready to renew the solemn promises and vows made by or for them at holy Baptism. They are to ratify and confirm these and in response they say, "I do." Then he asks them: "Do ye promise to follow Jesus Christ as your Lord and Saviour?" (which faith and following, we may note, is surely the very heart of the Christian religion and the essential core of what it is to know God).

Following responsive versicles from the Psalter, there is an ancient prayer, offered by the bishop for those about to be confirmed. It is informed by Isaiah 11:2 (not from the Latin or Hebrew but from the Greek transla-tion known as the Septuagint) where the seven (rather than six) gifts of the Holy Spirit are found. These are the spirit of wisdom and understanding, the spirit of counsel and ghostly strength, the spirit of knowledge and true godliness, and holy fear.

Commenting on the sevenfold gifts the late A. J. Mason made the follow-ing observations :

> None of the gifts are directly of moral virtue. They are
> gifts which set a man in a position to acquire moral vir-
> tues, and incline him to practice them; but they do not in
> any way supply him with virtues ready-made, or relieve
> their possessor from the necessity of carefully forming
> right habits of action and feeling. It seems that all the
> sanctifying work of the Holy Ghost is done by an inward
> teaching, which commends to us the true principles of
> moral choice, and an inward strengthening, by which the
> forces of Christ are imparted to us, that we may act, and
> act perseveringly, upon the convictions which the Holy
> Ghost has wrought in us. (*The Relation of Confirmation
> to Baptism*, 1891, p. 481.)

I would add that this is entirely what the New Testament leads us to expect and think, for the indwelling Spirit (whose work St. Paul so lovingly describes in Romans 8 and elsewhere) prompts, guides, and inspires us so that we may be and do what is pleasing to God. Only in this way of being treated as persons can we know God personally.

Though there is no required anointing with oil (chrism), the Bishop does lay his hands upon each person and calls upon the Lord to defend and empower his adopted child (through humble reliance upon the Spirit's presence and power) to live faithfully and come unto his everlasting kingdom. And following the Lord's Prayer there are two prayers before the Blessing. In the first, the bishop prays thus:

> Let thy fatherly hand, we beseech thee, ever be over them; let thy Holy Spirit ever be with them; and so lead them in the knowledge and obedience of thy Word, that in the end they may obtain everlasting life....

Like other confirmed Christians the newly confirmed are now to walk under the protection of God and in the power of his Spirit as they prayerfully meditate upon, and thereby are prepared for obedience to, the written Word of God. Knowledge of the Word is the route into the knowing of God the Father through Jesus Christ, the Word made flesh. And, as we shall see, this knowledge is increased through the use of the Daily Offices of Morning and Evening Prayer (see chapter six) and is enhanced and made corporate and personal in the reception of Holy Communion (see chapter eight).

## BAPTISM BUT NOT HOLY BAPTISM!

There seems to be little doubt but that there is a direct route from "The Service of Holy Baptism" (pp. 299ff.) of the 1979 Prayer Book of the Episcopal Church to its major innovations in sexuality of 2003–5 (e.g., the acceptance of an active homosexual bishop).

I recall vividly a meeting of the Standing Liturgical Commission at the General Convention of 2000, where I was giving evidence on behalf of seeking permission to use the classic *BCP* of 1928 in parishes. It was agreed that with the local bishop's specific permission, and under certain conditions, certain services of the 1928 *BCP* could be used. However, of one thing all present seemed clear, and this was that there was no substitute possible for the use of the Baptismal Service in the 1979 Book. For herein was contained what they obviously believed was an essential part of the progressive religion of the modernized Episcopal Church.

Turning to the Service itself, the first sentence of the introductory comments begins: "Holy Baptism is full initiation ...." Here, a word that belongs chiefly to the human sciences such as anthropology and culture-studies, and that the Early Church used rarely of Baptism, takes pride of place to describe what is baptism in the Episcopal Church (and other liberal denominations). It is the ritual entrance into "the Christian community", which, as was noted above, is the coming together of "individuals" for a common purpose.

But what kind of community? This is presented within what is called "The Baptismal Covenant" which is the center of the service, and is more like a contract between a senior and junior partner, than a Covenant where God alone establishes it and calls repentant sinners into it. We find that, though there is a promise to be committed to certain traditional things such as church attendance, resisting of evil, and proclaiming the Gospel, there is also a commitment to a modern thing. The innovation is seen in the questions which require an affirmative reply. They are: "Will you seek and serve Christ in all persons, loving your neighbor as yourself?" And , "Will you strive for justice and peace among all people and respect the dignity of every human being?"

Anyone who has followed the debates and resolutions of the General Convention from the 1960s through to 2003 will have no doubt of the great importance attached to this innovation, which provided titles and themes for not a few Conventions after 1979. What these came to mean—if we listen to the General Convention and the Executive Council—is a virtually total dedication to the expanding agenda of civil and human rights and the support of all moves to affirm self-worth and human dignity. That is, to a serious dumbing-down of orthodox doctrine and biblical morality and to the adopting of an "enlightened" modern approach, where doctrine is based on contemporary experience of life (or of God in life). Thus, from the standpoint of the Liturgical Commission, anyone making these commitments, within the context of the modern Episcopal Church, is virtually committing himself/herself in principle to all the innovations introduced by the General Convention since the 1960s, from the right to divorce and remarriage in church, through a variety of women's and minority rights, to the rights of homosexual persons to be true to their "orientation." That is, a commitment to "a Christian community," which seems here to be not only in the world and for the world but also of the world, differing only, it appears, from the world ("enlightened culture") in using "God-language" for human ideas and activity.

In the traditional Services of Holy Baptism, the emphasis is upon regeneration, birth from above, and dying to sin and rising to new life in Christ, for the purpose of membership of a heavenly communion (not an earthly, activist community), where life on earth is a pilgrimage toward the heavenly Jerusalem, and where, as a soldier and servant of Christ, the baptized believer is at war with the world, the flesh, and the devil, doing the will of the heavenly Father. It is entry into a permanent relation with the Father through the Lord Jesus Christ by the Holy Ghost for eternal life. Let my reader compare the content of the 1979 service with that in the *BCP* of 1662 or 1928 in order to get the complete contrast between the doctrine, style, and emphases as well as the content of the two different forms of entrance into Christian faith and life. As with most examples of modern Liturgy, there is sufficient traditional material in the 1979 Baptismal Service to hide from those who do not look carefully its real and true purpose of initiating people into an activist community—which, in the name of God, is primarily committed to reflecting social, cultural, and economic change in human society, so that in this world equality, justice, and peace are to be found, and war and discrimination against persons pass away.

# 6

For Christians the privilege, obligation, and tradition of daily prayer are traced not only to the Jewish discipline adopted and developed by the early Church but to Jesus himself. As a boy he was taught the Jewish custom of praying three times a day. The morning prayer consisted of the meditative recital of the *Shema* (Deut. 6:4–7) which confesses the Unity of the LORD our God and the duty to love him, and the *Tephilla*, a prayer made up of eighteen acts of blessing God (benedictions)—e.g. "Blessed art thou, O Lord, God of Abraham … " The afternoon prayer required only the *Tephilla* while the evening prayer was the same as morning prayer. Of course the use of the *Shema* and *Tephilla* was the minimum, not the maximum, and along with them the pious Jew prayed the Psalter and offered his own petitions. Jesus obviously used the discipline of daily prayer and in using it made it the means of communion with his Father in heaven, for at the age of twelve he told his mother, "I must be about my Father's business" (Luke 2:49).

The Anglican services of Morning and Evening Prayer, sometimes called Matins and Evensong and referred to as the Daily Offices, the Choir Offices, and the Divine Office, are directly descended from the system of daily services or Canonical Hours of the medieval Church. The latter developed from the simple morning and evening prayer of the early Church and are to be found in the Breviaries used by the monastic and secular clergy.

It is generally recognized that the creation of Morning and Evening Prayer in the sixteenth century was an important advance in engaging the laity in the duty and joy of daily worship and prayer. And in this provision the name of Archbishop Thomas Cranmer is recognized as a literary genius. The late Massey H. Shepherd, Jr., put it well when he wrote:

> It was the genius of the great Reformers, such as Luther and Cranmer, to see the potential advantage to the Church of making the Daily Offices a means of corporate worship for all the faithful, the laity as well as the clergy, and, in particular, a vehicle for the recovery of a knowledge of the Holy Scriptures by all the people of God. To achieve these ends required not only the translation of the offices into the vernacular, but a very practical simplification and reduction in both the number of these offices and their content. The artistry of Cranmer's accomplishment of these purposes has been the admiration of all

succeeding generations. (*The Oxford American Prayer Book Commentary*, 1950, Introduction, p. 1.)

We certainly admire the literary artistry. At the same time we are also grateful to God that the daily services can and were intended to be, under the blessing of God, a wonderful vehicle for the knowledge of God through the encounter with him through his Word and in prayer.

In *Prayer Book Studies VI* published in 1957 the Standing Liturgical Commission of the Episcopal Church stated:

> The genius of our Common Prayer is in no instance more clearly exemplified than in the Daily Offices of Morning and Evening Prayer. Out of the elaborate, complicated Canonical Hours of the medieval Breviary the sixteenth-century Reformers produced a pattern of daily praise and prayer that was loyal to tradition, solidly Scriptural in content, simple and convenient in execution, balanced and artful in design. The older Latin Offices had been a primary duty of the clergy, the monks and friars, upon whom their recitation was imposed by canonical law. But the Reformers intended their simpler, vernacular forms to be a means of corporate worship and edification in the knowledge of God's Word for all the laity no less than the clergy. In this purpose their labors have borne abundant fruit. To no other part of the Prayer Book have the lay people shown greater attachment and responsiveness. (page 32)

It is perhaps impractical to expect all faithful Anglicans to go twice daily to their parish church in order to say and/or sing the Daily Office. However, there is no reason why either or both of the services should not be used in the home as the basis for personal and/or family prayers. Alternatively, church members who live near each other can gather in homes on a regular basis to pray one or both of these offices. Where there is a desire and a will to pray them, a way will certainly be found to do so.

## THE LOGIC OF THE SERVICES

The daily services are for the covenant people of God, the disciples of Jesus Christ, and those who walk by faith in faithfulness—or at least desire so to do. Thus Morning Prayer and Evening Prayer begin with a call from God through his minister to his people to engage in penitence, praise, thanksgiving, instruction from God through his Word, and petitionary prayer. This call is achieved through the recital of sentences from Scripture and an Exhortation, which fully recognizes both the sinfulness of the human condition before God and the generosity of the God who issues the call.

Having been summoned and having come before Almighty God as believers or people of Christian faith, the covenant people of God must confess their sins, recognizing that in and of themselves they have nothing good to offer unto their gracious, faithful, covenant Lord who is the God of all mercy. So kneeling down and thereby symbolically submitting to the sovereign mercy of God, his people confess not only their rebellion against him ("we have offended against thy holy laws"), but the actual sinfulness of their souls ("there is no health in us").

The Declaration of divine absolution and remission of sins pronounced by the priest or bishop is composed of a medley of scriptural sentences. To all who repent of their sins and believe the promises of the Gospel there is full and free forgiveness, even as there is also a call to "be pure and holy," for faith works by love and issues in good works.

The rest of the service may be described as an expression of responsive faith. The faith which has responded to God's call and heard his promise of forgiveness and eternal life now speaks to God and hears from him. It is entirely fitting and appropriate therefore that believers begin their response by saying the prayer composed by our Lord himself, the Lord's Prayer, which is the model for all prayer and, when prayed in sincerity and truth, a perfect expression of prayer. And following this the mind, having descended into the heart, and warmed by God's gracious presence and word, is ready to praise his name. This is done through the versicles taken from Psalm 51:15 which lead into the *Gloria Patri* or the "little doxology": "Glory to the Father and to the Son and to the Holy Ghost … " Christian souls are now ascending in and with Christ to heaven by the presence of the Holy Ghost to bow before and adore the Father, in the Name and through the mediation of the Son. They not only affirm Trinitarian Theism but they worship this LORD God, who is the Blessed, Holy, and Undivided Trinity of the Father, the Son, and the Holy Ghost.

Responsive faith continues to praise the Lord through the *Venite* (Ps. 95) which celebrates the Majesty of God, the Creator, Sustainer, Provider, and Judge. Then follows the meditative reading or chanting of the appointed psalms. These are prayed in, with, and through Jesus Christ, and not merely as prayers from the Old Testament (see below chapter seven for a full treatment of the use of the Psalter). This contemplative, reflective hearing is continued with the listening to what God has to say and teach from the first lesson, read from the Old Testament. It is heard not merely as a reading but as a lesson (i.e., a teaching from God himself through the illumination of the Holy Spirit on the mind).

Having heard the Word of God read, the congregation of Christ's flock joins again in the worship and praise of Almighty God. This is achieved through the use of the *Te Deum laudamus* (the magnificent hymn of praise to the Father, the Son, and the Holy Ghost) or the shorter *Benedictus es, Domine* (from the addition to the Book of Daniel in the Apocrypha) or the longer *Benedicite, omnia opera Domini* (from the same source as the *Benedictus*).

God has yet more to say unto his believing people, and so there is read the Second Lesson, this time from the New Testament, again to be heard with obedient, reflective faith. Following it, there is again the praise of God through the chanting or recital of either the *Benedictus* (the Song of Zechariah, father of John the Baptist) or Psalm 100, the *Jubilate Deo*.

At this stage, praising, believing souls are ready to speak to God and tell him what they believe as baptized Christians on the basis of his Revelation to them through sacred Scripture. Thus they join in the Apostles' Creed, each one making his or her personal profession of faith, "I believe" in unison to show that this is the response of the Bride to the Bridegroom, an echoing of what he has revealed to his Bride. On some occasions they may use the longer and more theologically developed confession of faith, the Nicene Creed. The Creed is a word addressed to God, a word shared with fellow Christians, and a concise word of hope and good news offered to the world.

Finally, as forgiven, praising, and believing souls, worshippers express their faith and commitment to Jesus as Lord by engaging in petitionary and intercessory prayers for themselves and others, especially those with heavy responsibilities in State and Church. They pray for others in the confidence that the Lord God who has blessed them will also bless those for whom they pray. They pray in the name of the Lord Jesus to the Father in heaven, in the power of the Holy Ghost The set prayers, which are all memorable in style and theology, include the two great prayers which all mature Anglicans ought to know by heart—the Prayer for all Conditions of Men and the General Thanksgiving. The final prayer of the service is the Grace, taken straight from the Bible (2 Cor. 13:14).

Such is the logic of faith of Morning Prayer—and the same logic is there in Evening Prayer. Modern usage often begins the Office at the Versicles and thereby destroys the logic of faith which requires us to begin where we are, in our sin, in order to rise by and in Christ as forgiven people to the praise of God Almighty. This is why in the Common Prayer Tradition the confession of sin is not optional! Such is the human condition, even of the best of us, that we always need to confess our sins of commission and omission, and to recognize both the bias to sin which is deep in our souls and our participation in the sins of mankind as a whole. There is an exception to this general rule as when the Order for Holy Communion is to be celebrated immediately after Morning Prayer, since there is a full penitential section in that Order.

One important dimension of the Daily Office, often mentioned by the saints of God in their writings, is that it is the voice of the bride addressing her Bridegroom, and it is the very prayer which Christ himself, in and through his Body, addresses to the Father. Thus, by offering praise to God in heaven, the Church on earth joins in the heavenly litany and canticles of praise of the angels and archangels. Earth and heaven combine in the heavenly liturgy.

Intimately connected on earth to the Daily Office is the Litany or General Supplication. It is to be used after the Third Collect of Morning or Evening Prayer on certain days (see the rubrics). The Litany is composed of (a) solemn addresses to the Holy Trinity; (b) petitions for deliverance from evil; (c) entreaties addressed to the Lord Jesus recalling his saving deeds for us; (d) petitions and intercessions ending with the "O Lamb of God … ", the "Lord have mercy" and the Lord's Prayer, and (e) a final supplication, composed of responsive versicles and collects. The entire Litany, apart from the beginning and the ending is addressed to the Lord Jesus.

The aim of all prayer is to know God, and thus the Litany ends with this prayer:

> We humbly beseech thee, O Father, mercifully to look upon our infirmities; and for the glory of thy Name, turn from us all those evils that we most justly have deserved; and grant, that in all our troubles we may put our whole trust and confidence in thy mercy, and evermore trust thee in holiness and pureness of living, to thy honour and glory; through our only Mediator and Advocate, Jesus Christ our Lord. Amen.

To know God is to live in utter dependence upon his mercy and strength.

# MEDITATIVE PARTICIPATION

Faith hears and reads Scripture as the Word of God. Therefore it hears prayerfully and meditatively. This spirit is captured in Psalm 19, "Let the words of my mouth and the meditation of my heart, be alway acceptable in thy sight, O LORD, my strength and my redeemer" (verse 14). It is stated with clarity in the Collect for the Second Sunday in Advent:

> Blessed Lord, who hast caused all holy Scriptures to be written for our learning; grant that we may in such wise hear them, read, mark, learn, and inwardly digest them, that by patience and comfort of thy holy Word, we may embrace and ever hold fast, the blessed hope of everlasting life, which thou hast given us in our Saviour Jesus Christ. Amen.

This Collect assumes what the Church of God has always believed, that the Holy Bible is the record, inspired by the Holy Spirit, of God's self-revelation to human beings. Further, it assumes that it was written under God's superintendence for our benefit, that we may learn therein, through the illumination of our minds by the Holy Spirit, of the nature of God and of his salvation offered to us in Jesus, the Christ. To hear or read Scripture prayerfully and in faith is to place oneself in the position to be taught by God, where the Lessons become truly teaching sessions of the Holy Ghost.

In the Collect, we pray that we may hear the Lessons (that is, hear not only with our physical ears, but also with the spiritual ears of our soul and thus allow the Word of God to enter our minds and hearts and wills); that we may mark them (that is, notice the particular message or teaching, doctrinal, moral, or spiritual which God is giving us through the Lesson); that we may learn (that is, take to heart to be obeyed and learn off by heart in order to meditate upon later, where appropriate); and that we may inwardly digest them (that is, allow the teaching of the Word of God to become food for our souls through our inward receiving of its contents in the mind, with the affections, and by the will). By such receiving of the Word of God we gain knowledge about and grow in the knowing of the living God and thus we embrace and hold fast "the blessed hope of everlasting life" through Jesus Christ.

In my book, *Meditating as a Christian* (Harper-Collins, 1991) I made a distinction between informative reading and formative reading, as a way to state the nature of biblical meditation which is possible in the Daily Office (and, of course, at other times as well). Most of the reading we do is to gain information—from newspaper, book, letter, report, journal, and magazine. The information may be for work or leisure or another purpose. Now to read the Bible for information, that is informatively, is to study it as a historical, religious book. Biblical Studies in the seminary are usually sophisticated forms of informative reading. The professor is here in charge and looks at the Book as an object which he or she is examining.

In contrast, formative reading is to read in such a way as to be formed by what is read. It is to read slowly, preferably aloud, so that the Word can be seen, heard, and tasted. It is also to read prayerfully and expectantly. In this approach the intention is to put Jesus Christ in charge so that he can speak to the reader and hearer through the Word and by the Spirit. To read and hear in this way in the Daily Office is an art to be cultivated and cannot be achieved overnight. To develop the art may require returning to the Lessons at the end of the Office and re-reading them in the formative mode. Or it may require preparing for their reading in the Office by looking at them or studying them in advance. At first it may only be possible to treat one of the Lessons seriously. We must begin where we are and grow in grace and in the knowledge of God, for God is a tender Father who leads us on by his gracious hand.

REPETITION

One of the aims of modern Liturgy, with its multiple options, appears to be to keep people from staying with one form of worship, one set of texts and prayers. However, there is great spiritual benefit in the use of the same texts day by day, especially if they are, as in the Daily Office, excellent Canticles and Prayers in fine, memorable English. However, this benefit only applies if they are said, sung, or prayed in faith with the mind in the heart. They will become utterly boring if they are merely repeated because that is what is required. To the heart which is seeking to know and love God they become the very words through which that knowledge and faith is expressed. Familiarity with them increases their usefulness as the content of the human response to God's gracious invitation to draw near to him and behold his glory.

If they are learned off by heart, then each day as they are prayed, the mind is able both to see and to pour into them ever deeper meaning; the affections are able to be raised in delight, peace, and love towards God, while the will is moved in resolve to obey God at all times. Further, the stability of the structure of fixed Canticles and Prayers provides the appropriate context for the changing Psalms and Lessons. The latter can be appreciated, and their content spiritually received, because of the devotional and theological reliability of the structure in which they are placed.

In fact the logic of faith, which we have noticed informing Daily Prayer, is the logic of the whole of Common Prayer. We are summoned by God to daily prayer to hear his Word, utter his praise, offer prayers and supplications, and be strengthened for our vocation in daily life. We are further summoned to the Lord's Table each Sunday, the first day of the week and the day of the Resurrection of the Lord, in order to meet him in Word and Sacrament—in the most spiritually intimate communion as we hear again his Word and receive his Body and Blood.

The daily lectionary and the Eucharistic lectionary are also harmonized by this logic of faith. A lectionary is an ordered program of readings from Scripture for the public worship of the Church. The daily lectionary for the offices has the basic aim to take the Church through the whole Bible each year, and through the New Testament more thoroughly. Its origins as a system are in the mid-sixteenth century. In contrast, the lectionary for use in the Order for Holy Communion for Sundays (and the week after) and holy Days, is particularly selected to reflect the Christian Year, and its origins are in the fourth and fifth centuries. All this is to say that by such lectionary arrangement the Church consciously puts herself under the rule and authority of Scripture. (For the Lectionary actually printed in *the Book of Common Prayer*, the Eucharistic Lectionary, see the chapter on Holy Communion.)

## NOT ONLY SAYING BUT ALSO SINGING

The long tradition of the use of the Daily Office in the West, and thus in the daily worship of *Ecclesia Anglicana*, included chanting and singing unto the Lord. The use of singing and music continued in the Church of England, even as the services were provided in English not Latin from the middle of the sixteenth century, and as they were shortened to make them accessible to laity as well as to clergy and religious. Parts of the *The Book of the Common Prayer* (1549), following the Litany provided in English in 1544, were given a monophonic setting by John Merbecke in 1550. Thus there was from the beginning of the Reformed Church of England, and what we call Anglicanism, the possibility that the daily worship of the English Church in its cathedrals, parishes and college chapels could be offered to the Lord both in speech and in song. And, a little later, a polyphonic equivalent was developed for the English services and this gave rise to what is now called "Anglican chant." However, Merbecke's basically simple settings were revived in the nineteenth century and they are still in use, especially at Holy Communion.

Anyone who wishes to see the basic provision of traditional liturgical music for use with the traditional Common Prayer needs to consult a book such as *The Choral Service. The Liturgical Music for Morning and Evening Prayer, the Litany and the Holy Communion* (H. W. Gray Company, New York, 1927). Here there is clear advice on which parts of Morning and Evening Prayer should be said, and which parts sung, and also how the parts to be sung should actually be sung.

Of course, a congregation usually needs to be led by a competent organist and choir, if the offering of praise and prayer in song is truly to be a satisfactory spiritual sacrifice unto the Lord. And this remains true if the music used is not traditional but a modern composition in, for example, a style such as that of Taizé. After all, the Lord Jesus provides the gift of making music in the Spirit, even as he also provides the gift of proclaiming his word.

Perhaps the point needs to be made that, although the liturgical texts of Common Prayer belong in their English form to the sixteenth and seventeenth centuries, the music to go with them, as long as it truly serves the purpose of encouraging reverence before God, can be as contemporary as desired. Further, the choice of hymns, and the place in the service where they are used, is to be regarded as a serious matter, if they are to serve the purpose of truly helping the congregation come to know the Lord and be known by him There is no actual place for them within the Order for Morning or Evening Prayer itself, for within the Office there are the Psalms, Canticles, and Versicles to be sung, whenever possible. However, hymns can be used with spiritual benefit to begin the service (as a processional), before and after the homily, and as a suitable means to end the service (recessional).

## ADVICE FROM WILLIAM BEVERIDGE

Writing nearly three hundred years ago William Beveridge, Bishop of St Asaph in Wales, gave some first-class advice on how to prepare for, and participate in, corporate worship. Here is part of what he wrote in *The Great Necessity and Advantage of Public Prayer*, 1708:

Here then is the great task we have to do in all our

public devotions, even to keep our spirits or hearts in a right posture all the while that we are before God, who sees them, and takes special notice of their motions … Blessed be God, by his assistance we may do it, if we will but set ourselves in good earnest about it, and observe these few rules ….

First, when you go to the house of God at the hour of prayer, be sure to leave all worldly cares and business behind you, entertaining yourselves, as ye go along, with these, or such like sentences of Scripture: *Like as the hart desireth the waterbrooks, so longeth my soul after thee, O God; my soul is athirst for God, yea, even the living God. When shall I come to appear before the presence of God?* (Ps. 42:1–2). *O how amiable are thy dwellings, thou Lord of hosts! My soul hath a desire and longing to enter into the courts of the Lord. My heart and my flesh rejoice in the living God.* (Ps. 84:1–2). *We will go into his tabernacle and fall low on our knees before his footstool.* (Ps. 132:7).

When ye come into the church say with Jacob, *How dreadful is this place! This is none other but the house of God; and this is the gate of heaven* (Gen. 28:17), or something to that purpose. And as soon as ye can get an opportunity, prostrate yourselves upon your knees before the Master of the house, the great God of heaven, humbly beseeching him to unite your hearts unto himself, to cleanse your thoughts by the inspiration of his Holy Spirit, to open your eyes, and to manifest himself unto you, and to assist you with such a measure of grace in offering up these *spiritual sacrifices*, that they may be *acceptable* to him by Jesus Christ.

And now set yourselves, in good earnest, as in God's sight, keeping your eye only upon him, looking upon him as observing what you think, as well as what you say or do, all the while you are before him.

While one or more of the *Sentences* out of God's Holy Word (wherewith we very properly begin our Devotions to him) are *reading*, apprehend it as spoken by God himself at first, and now repeated in your ears, to put you in mind of something, which he would have you to believe or do upon this occasion.

While the *Exhortation* is reading, hearken diligently to it, and take particular notice of every word and expression in it, as contrived on purpose to prepare you for the service of God, by possessing your minds with a due sense of his special presence with you, and of the great ends of your coming before him at this time.

While you are confessing your sins with your mouth, be sure to do it also in your hearts, calling to mind every one, as many as he can, of those particular sins which he hath committed, either by doing what he ought not to do, or not doing what he ought, so as to repent sincerely of them, and steadfastly resolve never to commit them any more.

While the minister is pronouncing the *Absolution* in the name of God, every one should lay hold upon it for himself, so as firmly to believe, that upon true repentance, and faith in Christ, he is now discharged and absolved from all his sins, as certainly as if God himself had declared it with his own mouth, as he hath often done it before, and now, by his ministers.

While you, together with the minister, are repeating the *Psalms* or *Hymns*, to the honour and glory of God, observe the minister's part as well as your own; and lift up your hearts, together with your voices, to the highest pitch you can, in acknowledging, magnifying and praising the infinite wisdom, and power, and goodness, and glory of the most high God in all his works, the wonders that he hath done, and still doth, for the children of men, and for you among the rest.

While God's *Word* is read in either of the chapters, whether of the *Old* or *New Testament,* receive it not as the word of men but (as it is in truth) the Word of God, which effectually worketh in you that believe (1 Thess. 2:13). And therefore *hearken* to it with the same attention, reverence and faith, as you would have done, if you had stood by Mount Sinai, when God proclaimed the Law, and by our Saviour's side, when he published the Gospel.

While the *Prayers* or *Collects* are reading, although you ought not to repeat them aloud, to the disturbance of other people; yet you must repeat them in your hearts, your minds accompanying the minister from one prayer to another, and from one part of each prayer to the other, all along with affection suitable to the matter sounding in your ears, humbly adoring God according to the names, properties or works, which are attributed to him at the beginning of each *Prayer*, earnestly desiring the good things which are asked him in the body of it, for yourselves or others. And steadfastly believing in Jesus Christ for his granting of them, when he is named, as he is at the end of each prayer, except that of *St Chrysostom*; because that is directed immediately to Christ himself as promising, that *when two or three are gathered together in his name, he will grant their requests*, which is therefore very properly put at the end of all our daily prayers, and also the *Litany* (most part whereof is directed also to our Saviour) that when we have made all our *common supplications* unto him, we may act our faith in him again for God's granting of them according to his said promise. And so we may be dismissed with, *The Grace of our Lord Jesus Christ, the Love of God the Father, and the Communion or Fellowship of the Holy Ghost*; under which are comprehended all the blessings, that we can have, or can desire, to make us completely happy, both now and for ever.

After the *Blessing*, it may be expedient still to continue for some time upon your knees, humbly beseeching Almighty God to pardon what he hath seen amiss in you, since you came into his presence; and that he would be graciously pleased to hear the prayers, and to accept of the praises, which you have offered up unto him, through the merits of Jesus Christ our only Mediator and Advocate.

Certainly the Psalter is at the very heart of the Daily Office. It is the inspired collection of prayers which the Church prays with and in Christ and which the individual Christian prays as a member of the Church, the Body of Christ. Today it is not easy for Christians, who have had little or no instruction in liturgical prayer and who have not been taught how the Church over the centuries has used the Psalms, to pray them as Christians. Certainly it is difficult to pray them in this manner if the only encounter with them is as a Gradual (appointed psalm verses to be sung or read between scripture readings); modern Episcopalians seem only to encounter the Psalter through the ten or so verses from one psalm between the Old Testament and New Testament readings in the modern Eucharist. Further, it is nearly impossible to pray the Psalms as Christian prayers using the dynamic equivalency and inclusivist translations which are in recent Prayer Books, as well as in the New Revised Standard Version and other recent English versions of the Bible.

We need to bear in mind that we do not use the Psalter as if it were only an ancient Jewish book of prayers which were said or sung in the Temple, synagogue, and home. Of course there is a legitimate, and for us today, necessary academic study which attempts to analyze the Psalter and to determine the original use and meaning of each of the Psalms in the worship and religious experience of Israel. In particular, there has been valuable work done on establishing the nature of the Hebrew poetry, which uses a variety of parallel arrangements of lines, as well as in associating particular psalms with specific festivals in Israel. Such study is what Old Testament scholars engage in and seminarians learn. The fruit of some of this study can be, and has been, assimilated and used profitably within the Church to aid her Liturgy and the prayers of her members. It belongs to what I called the informative reading of the Bible: yet obviously here it is scholarly, sophisticated, informative reading.

However, Christians have consistently used the Psalter formatively, following the way in which the Jews themselves used it before and in the time of Jesus. In Hebrew the Psalms are called *Tehillim*, "songs of praise"; in Greek they are called *Psalmoi*, "songs to be sung to the sound of the harp." Since they are inspired by God, they have a timeless quality. In praying the psalms, devout Jews thought of the psalms as prayers which are always relevant and always contemporary. They were and are always the prayer of Israel, or of the individual Israelite. They saw in the inspired verse of the psalms not only their praises and thanksgivings, laments and complaints, petitions and intercessions, hopes and joys, but also their prayer for the Messiah, the Deliverer of Israel. The Psalter was God's provision of prayer for his people to use in temple, synagogue, and home. Since it had been inspired by his Spirit, the LORD was committed by his gracious covenant relation with Israel to hear those who prayed in its spirit and words.

Jesus, the Jew, entered into this tradition of daily praying the "songs of praise" which the Spirit of the Lord had inspired king David and others to compose. He saw his vocation in the first psalm—"Blessed is the man ... whose delight is in the law of the LORD and in his law doth he meditate day and night." In the portraits and prophecies of the Messiah (e.g. Psalms 2, 72, & 110) Jesus saw his Messianic role as the anointed suffering King of Israel. We may claim that the Psalter was the Prayer Book of Jesus for the whole of his life: He quoted it in his public ministry, and from it He prayed as he died on the Cross ("My God, my God, why hast thou forsaken me?", Psalm 22). He expired with a part of Psalm 31 on his lips: "Into thy hands I commend my spirit." Then, as the resurrected Lord, he met his disciples and explained to them what was written concerning him not only in the Law and the Prophets but also in the Psalms (Luke 24:44).

Against this background, it was entirely to be expected that the first Christians would also use the Psalter and imitate their Lord's praying of it. They wanted to pray in the words inspired by the Holy Spirit as God's covenant people had long done. Thus we find that in the early Church the Psalms were prayed (said or sung) as the prayers of the new Israel whose Messiah and Lord is Jesus of Nazareth, the exalted King. Nearly fifty Psalms are cited in the New Testament, and there they are invested with a Christian interpretation. This tradition of use and meaning is to be seen not only in the place of the Psalter in the emerging Liturgy of the Church, but also in the commentaries on the Psalter by such well-known bishops as Augustine of Hippo, Chrysostom, Hilary and Ambrose, not to mention Jerome to whom we owe the Latin Vulgate.

In the Introduction to the Divine Office of the Roman Catholic Church we receive this wonderful advice:

> Whoever says the psalms in the name of the Church should pay attention to the full meaning of the Psalms, especially that messianic understanding which led the Church to adopt the Psalter. The messianic meaning is made completely manifest in the New Testament; it is in fact declared by Christ our Lord ... Following this path,

*the Fathers took the whole Psalter and explained it as a prophecy about Christ and his Church; and for this same reason psalms were chosen for the sacred liturgy. Even if certain artificial interpretations were sometimes accepted, generally both the Fathers and the liturgy rightly heard in the psalms Christ calling out to his Father, or the Father speaking to the Son; they even recognized in them the voice of the Church, the apostles and martyrs ... This christological interpretation in no way refers only to those psalms which are considered messianic but also extends to many in which without doubt there are mere appropriations. Such appropriations, however, have been commended by the tradition of the Church.*

In the worship of the Church the Christian interpretation and use of the Psalter has been made clear through the use of several aids: namely, the headings before each psalm, antiphons (a phrase or line which indicates the theme), psalm collects (which summarize the Christian meaning for the worshippers), and the use of the Gloria at the end.

To pray the Psalter in this traditional, Christian, and Catholic way is exceedingly difficult for those who have only known and examined the Psalter through modern academic study. It seems such an irrational thing to the modern, secular mind to move from considering the Psalter only as the Jewish holy book and religious poetry of a pre-modern, near-eastern patriarchal society, to praying its contents in a wholly spiritual and Christ-centered manner as the Body of Christ in the twenty-first century. Yet the logic of faith (which confesses the centrality and Lordship of Jesus) calls us to do just this. This call can be made because the Psalter was written under the inspiration of the Holy Spirit: thus God knew the greater purpose to which he would put it even though king David and other writers could not see into the long-term plan of God, when they expressed their faith and convictions in Hebrew centuries ago.

Certainly in the 150 Psalms are mirrored the ideals of religious piety and communion with God, of sorrow for sin and the search for perfection, of walking unafraid in darkness by the lamp of faith: of obedience to the law of God, delight in the worship of God, fellowship with the friends of God, reverence for the word of God; of humility under the chastening rod, trust when evil triumphs and wickedness prospers, and serenity in the midst of storm. It is not surprising that the psalms of praise and lament can so easily become the prayer of honest, believing people today—be that prayer for themselves or for others. The Psalms inform our minds, warm our hearts, and direct our wills towards the knowledge of God. Yet, without denying this practical use of the Psalter, the logic of faith calls upon Christians to know a deeper level of experience—to pray each Psalm through, in, and with Christ, within his Body.

Used in this Christian way, the Psalms have advantages which no fresh compositions, however finely executed, can possibly have. Apart from their incomparable fitness to express our deep religious convictions and feelings, they are at the same time memorials of, and appeals to, former mercies and deliverances from God; they are acknowledgements of prophecies fulfilled; they point out the connection between the old and new dispensations (or administrations of God's covenant) and thereby teach us to admire and adore the wisdom of God displayed in both; further they provide us as we sing or say them with an inexhaustible variety of the noblest matter that can engage the meditations and contemplations of man.

PSALTER (1928)

What praying the Psalms with and in Jesus actually means we shall examine below. Here it is perhaps necessary to make a comment on the actual Psalter printed in *BCP* (1928). Its origin goes back as far as 1536, and it was made by Miles Coverdale from the Latin Vulgate Psalter, which was translated into Latin from Hebrew by the great scholar, Jerome, in the fifth century. Here it is important to note that the Latin translated the original and holy usage in the Church, which was then praying the Psalter in a Christ-centered way. By divine providence, the English translation captured this special character of the Vulgate, and, in doing so, it served, not primarily as an ancient Jewish text, but as the thoroughly naturalized Prayer Book of Christians as the People of God of David and the Lord Jesus.

It is of course possible to find modern translations of the Psalms which are superior to the Coverdale version in terms of technical accuracy; and it is also possible to find versions which communicate the power and beauty of the Hebrew poetic style in a clearer manner. Yet for Christian use, in order that the *Gloria* may truly be said in reverence and truthfulness at the end of each Psalm, we need a version which captures the authentic Christ-centered nature of this Jewish and Christian Prayer Book. Happily the 1928 Psalter can still do this for us: in contrast, the 1979 Psalter is ill suited for this holy purpose because of the modern, feminist ideology which informed its content.

Before we move on to look at the theme of Christ in the Psalms, it may be useful to recall how the Psalms were viewed by Anglican leaders of the last century. Here is what John Henry Hobart, Bishop of New York, wrote in his much-used *A Companion to the BCP* (1805). He wrote of the Coverdale Psalter as being a "more smooth and flowing" translation for church use than the Psalter in the *KJV*. Then he wrote:

> The Psalms were originally used in the service of the Jewish Temple and have been thence transferred into the Christian Church. These divinely inspired compositions breathe the sentiments of penitence, of prayer, and of praise, in strains most tender and sublime. By beautiful and interesting comparisons drawn from the works of nature and the customs of society, but principally by personal and ceremonial types and shadows, they display the excellence of Christian doctrine: the character, the offices, and the conditions of the Savior, and the circumstances of his Church and its members. As the Psalms therefore have a spiritual application and meaning, and are thus frequently applied by Christ and his apostles, it is no objection to the use of them that they contain sentiments and expressions applicable to the Jewish dispensation and to the particular circumstances of the king of Israel.

And he continued:

> Whatever the Psalmist says of the excellences of the law; of the ark, the temple, and the holy city of Jerusalem, of the sacrifices on the Jewish altar; and of his own distresses, his temporal enemies and signal deliverances, may be easily applied to the Gospel, which is the law fulfilled; to the Christian Church, which the ark, the temple and Jerusalem prefigured; to that one great sacrifice of Christ still commemorated in the holy Eucharist, from which the Jewish sacrifices derived all their efficacy; and to the humiliation of the Savior to the enemies of his Church and people, and to the victories by which he wrought their redemption; all which were set forth in the humiliation, the enemies, and the victories of the frequently distressed and persecuted, yet finally triumphant, king of Israel.

Bishop Hobart then proceeded to explain how Christians may use the "bitter imprecations of David against his enemies" when they are prayed with, in and through Christ. For Anglicans who wanted to know more of the principles which govern the Christian use and praying of the Psalms, he commended the Preface of Bishop George Horne's *Commentary on the Psalms*. Horne was Bishop of Norwich in England, and his commentary was much used in the early nineteenth century. I quote from it at the end of this chapter because, though historical study of the Psalms has continued, the Christian principles which guide the praying of the Psalms remain constant—simply because Jesus Christ is the same yesterday, today, and forever (Heb. 13:8). [See further: Patrick H. Reardon, "Christology and the Psalter: the Church's Christian Prayer Book," in *Creed & Culture*, ed. James H. Kushiner, Wilmington, Delaware, 2003.]

CHRIST IN THE PSALMS

In order to begin to appreciate how the apostolic Church read and prayed the Psalms, we need go no further than the fourth chapter of the Acts of the Apostles. Here we learn that Peter and John, who had been boldly preaching in Jerusalem the Gospel of the resurrected Messiah, the Lord Jesus, had been brought before the supreme law court of the Jews, the Sanhedrin, and told to stop preaching. On their release Peter and John returned to the fellowship of believers who began to praise the Lord in prayer.

> *They lifted up their voice to God with one accord and said, "Lord, thou art God, which hast made heaven and earth, and the sea, and all that in them is. Who by the mouth of thy servant David hast said, 'Why did the heathen rage and the people imagine vain things? The kings of the earth stood up, and the rulers were gathered together against the Lord and against his Christ.' [Ps. 2:1–2] For of a truth against thy holy child, Jesus, whom thou hast anointed, both Herod, and Pontius Pilate, with the Gentiles, and the people of Israel, were gathered together...."*

We notice that the early Christian fellowship, gathered in prayer, interprets the hostile kings and rulers of Psalm 2 in terms of Herod and Pontius Pilate, and the opposing "heathen" and "people" as the Gentiles (represented by the Roman empire), and the Jews. The "his Christ" or "his Anointed One" is understood as referring to Jesus himself (v. 27). The primitive, apostolic Church interpreted Psalm 2 not only as a prophecy concerning Jesus as the Messiah but also concerning the suffering of his ambassadors (Church) in the world as they proclaim His Gospel.

So it was that the Church came, by the example of Christ and through the illumination of his Spirit, to see in the Psalms both the vocation and experience of Christ and the vocation and experience of his Church. These are the two sides of the one divine coin and the two parts of one whole approach. The Psalter as a whole is the prayer of the Church as the Body of Christ and further, it is the prayer of both Head and Body (with all its members), that is of Christ and his brethren. The Epistle to the Hebrews teaches us to think of Christ as our exalted High Priest who as our Mediator in the presence of God is also our Intercessor there. When we pray in his name we are joined in the Spirit with his prayer, which he continually offers to the praise of God and for the good of his people. Thus to pray the Psalter, in and with him as his Body, is to be joined to him in his priestly, heavenly prayer.

Perhaps no one has expressed all this spiritual truth and insight more delightfully and accurately than St Augustine of Hippo in his famous *Commentary* or *Ennarations* on the Psalms. Here is what he wrote at the beginning of his commentary on Psalm 86. His train of thought is compact and thus needs to be read slowly and carefully, for it has reference not only to praying the Psalter but also to the whole Divine Office:

> *No greater gift could God have given to men than in making his Word, by which he created all things, their head, and joining them to him as his members: that the Son of God might become also the Son of man, one God with the Father, one Man with men; so that when we speak to God [the Father] in prayer for mercy, we do not separate the Son from him; and when the Body of the Son prays, it separates not its head from itself: and it is the one Saviour of his Body, our Lord Jesus Christ, the Son of God, who both prays for us, and prays in us, and is prayed to by us. He prays for us, as our Priest: He prays in us, as our Head; He is prayed to by us, as our God. Let us therefore recognize in him our words and his words in us.*

And a little later he said:

> *Therefore we pray to him, through him, in him; and we speak with him, and he speaks with us; we speak in him, he speaks in us the prayer of this psalm, which is entitled "A Prayer of David."*

So by means of the Psalter and in its inspired words we pray to the Father through the Son, and the Son prays in us to the Father.

In the rest of this chapter, we shall note first of all how the Psalms in Christian use become that prayer which rises from his Body (and each and every member) in and through Christ, our Head, to the Father; and then, secondly, we shall see how they are also the prayer of Christ, our heavenly Priest, both in us and for us.

Perhaps at this point I need to make clear (as I did in a chapter on the Psalms in my *Meditating as a Christian*) that it is wise for us today to build the spiritual, Christocentric reading of the Psalms on what is called the historical-grammatical study of them. Not all the Fathers felt this need; but we, living in a different world where the study of history is part of our cultural heritage and mindset, need to pay attention to the historical situation in Israel before we move on to the spiritual situation of the new Israel. Again it is a matter of the informative reading being done and then proceeding to the formative.

## IN AND THROUGH HIM

Jesus was a Jewish male, and thus in and through him, as members of his Body, we are united with his people, the Jews or Israelites. Israel's history and experience under the old covenant becomes through Jesus the history and experience of the Church under the new covenant. So it is foolish, to say the least, to omit the names Israel or Zion from the Psalter—as some modern church psalters do, for political reasons of not supporting the modern state of Israel. Our God is the God of Noah, Abraham, Moses, David and Elijah! And we read the record of God's dealings with the Israelites from the perspective of the fulfillment of the Old Testament by Jesus Christ. He came not to destroy the law of Moses and the contents of the prophecies of the Prophets, but to bring them to fulfillment. We assume that the New is in the Old concealed, the Old is by the New revealed, and Jesus Christ is the key to the Old Testament and the focus of the New.

The apostle Paul states this with his usual clarity when he calls the people of the new covenant by the term, "the Israel of God" (Gal. 6:17) and claims that this people has inherited the wonderful promises made to the old Israel (see Gal. 3:6ff. & 4:21ff.). However, he makes it clear in Romans 9 –11 that the Church is not the replacement of Israel but the embodiment of Israel until "the times of the Gentiles be fulfilled." The old Israel is the olive tree, many of whose branches have been cut off through unbelief; and the Church composed of the Gentile peoples is a wild olive grafted into the old olive tree, whose roots go down into Abraham. Being in the olive tree all the branches, both Jew and non-Jew (Gentile), are fed from the same trunk—thus their history is one, that of the Israel of God recorded in the Old Testament. So the Old Testament is the first part of the Christian Bible, and it is precisely this, the Christian Bible. Its only vital meaning for Christianity as a living religion in terms of the logic of faith is that meaning which Jesus, the Christ, gives it.

In practice, this means that in reading and praying the Psalms each day Christian believers interpret them through Christ, that is, in the light of the life, death, and resurrection of Jesus Christ and his teaching along with the teaching from his apostles. So, for example, there are not a few Psalms and parts of Psalms which praise God the Creator and Sustainer of the universe. By his almighty word each and every part of the cosmos is kept in being and motion (see e.g., Psalms 8, 19, 95, & 104) and everything he has made praises him. In the New Testament we learn that God the Father created and sustains the universe by the eternal Son (the eternal Word) and through the Holy Ghost (see John 1:3 & Col. 1:16). The Word which God utters and which both brings everything into being and keeps everything in being is the Son himself. So Christians allow this doctrinal teaching to enter their praying of the Psalms, and thus their use of them is in and through Christ. The created order reveals the glory of the Father, the Son and the Holy Ghost.

There is much in the Psalms about the history of the people and tribes of Israel. In particular, there is emphasis upon the Exodus from Egypt and, in a lesser manner, upon the Exile of the tribes in Babylon (see Psalms 95, 106, & 136). Included in the Exodus is the deliverance from bondage, the receiving of the Law at Sinai, the wilderness wanderings, and the final entry into Canaan, the land of promise and the land of milk and honey. Prayed in and with Christ, the Exodus points forward to the mighty act of God in the deliverance of his people through the Cross and Resurrection of Jesus: as the old covenant was brought into being by the Exodus so the new is created by the new Exodus of Calvary. The giving of the Law as the expression of the covenant relation at Sinai points to the giving of the new Law by Jesus on the hill in Palestine where he delivered the Sermon on the Mount (Matt. 5–7). Jesus is the new and greater Moses! The wanderings in the wilderness are the symbol of the journey both of the Church as the people in covenant with God and the Christian soul in a personal relation with God on the way to the kingdom of God in the age to come. And, finally, the promised land of milk and honey points to the goal of the earthly journey, the fullness of everlasting life in the beatific vision of God through Jesus Christ in heaven itself.

The Exile of the sixth century B.C. was an extremely painful experience for the tribes of Israel, for it led to the virtual loss of ten of them and the chastisement by God of the two which remained. The story is told in the last part of 2 Kings, and the pain is expressed in parts of the writings of the Prophets (e.g. in Jeremiah and Ezekiel). Psalm 79 captures this experience of horror and pain, "O God the heathen are come into thine inheritance; thy holy temple have they defiled." Praying such Psalms in Christ, the Church intercedes for those of its members who suffer for the cause of Christ and are persecuted for his name. It also enters into the pain resulting from chastisement when God chooses to purify his new covenant people through suffering on the way of sanctification. Thus in praying these Psalms one part of the Church of God identifies with and empathizes with another part, and in so doing enters into the union of Christ with his suffering disciples.

It is not surprising that the Psalms have much to say about the glorious Temple, built by Solomon, as the House of God and the city of Jerusalem, captured by his father, David, and called the "City of God." Psalms 24, 47, and 48 refer to the Temple on Mount Zion. Prayed through Christ, references to the Temple become pointers to the very Body of Jesus himself. (See John 2:21 where John tells us that Jesus spoke of his own Body as the new Temple of God, and see also 1 Corinthians 3:16–17 and 6:19 where Paul declares that the Church of the new covenant is the new Temple of the Holy Ghost.) God is present with and unto his new covenant people by his indwelling of them, and so, where they are gathered in the name of the Lord Jesus, there is God's own Temple. Further, the old city of Jerusalem on Mount Zion, to which Psalms 48 and 102 refer, points in Christ to the new Jerusalem which is the mother of the faithful (so Paul in Gal. 4:26) and which, according to the glorious vision of John in Revelation 21–22, is heaven itself with Christ as its very center (see also Heb. 12:22). Thus, prayed in Christ, Jerusalem is the Church of God, triumphant and perfected in Christ in heaven; it is also the very Church which is still militant with Christ against sin and death on earth. And within this context of understanding those Psalms (e.g., 113 to 118) which speak of the festivals and pilgrimages of Israel are used with reference to great festivals of the Church—Easter and Pentecost.

The Psalms which the devout have always found difficult to fit into this Christian use are the few which are often called the imprecatory Psalms (see e.g., 94 & 109), which call upon God to execute his vengeance upon the wicked and the enemies of Israel. Thus in some modern editions of the

Psalter such Psalms are sometimes omitted, or the parts of Psalms which are judged to breathe this vengeance are bracketed, so that they can be omitted. However, if the Church is praying these Psalms in and through Christ, she is praying them through the One whose sacrificial self-offering and Atonement absorbed the wrath of God against wickedness—in fact absorbed God's wrath against all sin. By Christ we are saved from the wrath of God (Rom.5:9). Therefore, while God must by his very holy nature be opposed to and punish all wickedness and evil, he has made it possible for sinners of all kinds to be saved from his wrath since he has provided the means in the sacrificial death of Jesus for his wrath to be turned into mercy towards repentant sinners. To pray these Psalms in Christ is to pray them through the very One whom God the Father "set forth to be a propitiation through faith in his blood" (Rom. 3:25). [On this subject of the cries for vengeance in the Psalter see for illuminating comment Derek Kidner, *Psalms 1–72*, Inter-Varsity Press, 1973, pp. 25–32, & Dietrich Bonhoeffer, *The Psalms. Prayer Book of the Bible*, SLG Press, Oxford, 1982, pp. 21–23.]

Of course, many of the Psalms easily become Christian prayers without too much meditative effort by those who use them (e.g. Psalms 27 & 28), for the Lord who is there named is known to Christians either as the Lord Jesus Christ or the One God, who is the Father, the Son, and the Holy Ghost. Then their accurate statement of the human condition and their cries to God for help and mercy convert quickly into the prayers of those believers who find themselves sorely tried and tempted in this world and are seeking God's help and guidance (e.g. Psalms 42 and 51) to live the Christian life. Further, the hymns of praise immediately become Christian hymns of praise (e.g. Psalms 33 and 111–113) as God is again understood as the One who is revealed and has acted in Jesus Christ, the Lord. And the Psalms (especially 119) which thank God for his Law and Word become testimonies and prayers to Jesus Christ, the Word made flesh and the giver of the new Law.

The experience of the centuries is that practice makes perfect! This approach to the Psalter takes time to develop and is a process of prayer which is never exhausted or completed in this life. Our Father is forever surprising his covenant children who pray to him as the Body of Christ in the prayers of the Psalter.

FROM THE SON TO THE FATHER

In the Psalter there is a set of Psalms which have been called the Royal

Psalms (see e.g., Psalms 2, 18, 20, 21 & 45). They are addressed to the king as petitionary prayers or thanksgivings; sometimes they express his prayer, or present a royal processional song or a bridal ode for his marriage. Within these Psalms the king is the "son of God"; and seemingly excessive claims are made for his reign and his kingdom. He is the "anointed one of the LORD" who will bring peace and justice to the world and save his own people.

Developing from the use Jesus himself and his apostles made of Psalm 110, which is the most quoted psalm in the New Testament (see its use in Matthew 22:41ff.), the early Church came to view this and the other messianic Psalms in terms of Christ calling out to the Father and/or the Father speaking to the Son. Psalm 110 has only seven verses but it is pregnant with meaning and begins with the LORD God telling the Messiah-King to sit at his right hand, the highest place of honor and majesty. The king is then promised by God that his enemies will become his footstool, and that he will rule over a willing, obedient people. Further, he will not only continue as king but as priest, with a unique priesthood, that of Melchizedek (for whom see Gen. 14:8 & Heb. 5:6ff; 7:1ff). Thus to read and pray these royal Psalms as prophecies of Christ in his relation to the Father is to enter by faith into the relation of the Son to the Father. It is to come to the Father in and through Jesus Christ and participate in an appropriately creaturely way both in his kingdom of grace and his communion with the Father.

To take a few examples from the royal Psalms. Originally Psalm 72 probably referred to Solomon as "the king's son"—David's son. In Christian use it became a prayer that the kingdom of the Son of God would extend over the whole earth—"yea, all kings shall fall down before him; all nations shall serve him." In contrast, Psalm 144 is a prayer of an Israelite king who gives thanks to God for victory in battle and then asks for blessings upon his people. In Christian use, it became the prayer of Christ thanking God the Father for his victory over sin, death, and hell and asking that his Church and kingdom would prosper.

Psalm 45 addresses in turn, the king, the Lord God, and then the new queen, in celebration of the marriage of the king to the queen. In Christian use, it was seen as portraying the mystical marriage between Christ, the Bridegroom, and the Church, the Bride (see Eph. 5:32).

Much more could be said about the Psalter but here is not the place to do so. I close this section with a Latin expression which captures the traditional Christian use of the Psalms: *semper in ore psalmus, semper in corde Christus* (always a psalm on the lips, always Christ in the heart).

# WISDOM FROM BISHOP GEORGE HORNE

Below are three quotations from the Preface to his *Commentary*; 1836 edition.]

1. [On the greatness of the Psalter]

The Psalms are an epitome of the Bible, adapted to the purposes of devotion. They treat occasionally of the creation and formation of the world; the dispensations of providence and the economy of grace; the transactions of the patriarchs; the exodus of the children of Israel; their journey through the wilderness and settlement in Canaan; their law, priesthood, and ritual; the exploits of their great men, wrought through faith; their sins and captivities; their repentances and restorations; the sufferings and victories of David; the peaceful and happy reign of Solomon; the advent of the Messiah with its effects and consequences; his incarnation, birth, life, passion, death, resurrection, ascension, kingdom, and priesthood; the effusion of the Spirit; the conversion of the nations; the rejection of the Jews; the establishment, increase and perpetuity of the Christian Church; the end of the world; the general judgment; the condemnation of the wicked, and the final triumph of the righteous with their Lord and King. These are the subjects here presented to our meditations.

We are instructed how to conceive of them aright, and to express the different affections, which, when so conceived of, they must excite in our minds. They are, for this purpose, adorned with the figures, and set off with all the graces of poetry; and poetry itself is designed yet farther to be recommended by the charms of music, thus consecrated to the service of God; that so delight may prepare the way for improvement, and pleasure become the handmaid of wisdom, while every turbulent passion is calmed by sacred melody, and the evil spirit is still dispossessed by the harp of the son of Jesse. This little volume, like the paradise of Eden, affords us in perfection, though in a miniature, everything that groweth elsewhere, "every tree that is pleasant to the sight and good for food:" and, above all, what was there lost, but is here restored, the tree of life in the midst of the garden. That which we read, as a matter of speculation, in other Scriptures, is reduced to practice, when we recite it in the Psalms; in those, repentance and faith are described, but in these, they are acted; by a perusal of the former, we learn how others served God, but, by using the latter, we serve him ourselves.

2. [Spiritual interpretation is open to over development and thus to be abused.]

That the spiritual interpretation of the Scripture, like all other good things, is liable to abuse, and that it hath been actually abused, both in ancient and modern days, cannot be denied. He who shall go about to apply, in this way, any passage, before he hath attained its literal meaning, may say what in itself is pious and true; but foreign to the text from which he endeavoureth to introduce it. St Jerome, it is well known, when grown older and wiser, lamented that, in the fervours of a youthful fancy, he had spiritualized the prophecy of Obadiah, before he understood (its historical, literal meaning). And it must be allowed, that a due attention to the occasion and scope of the Psalms would have pared off many unseemly excrescences, which now deform the commentaries of St Augustine and other Fathers, upon them. But these and other concessions of the same kind being made, as they are made very freely, men of sense will consider, that a principle is not therefore to be rejected, because it has been abused, since human errors can never invalidate the truths of God.

3. [On the Christian interpretation of the Psalms.]

As God is ever the same, and his doings uniform, his conduct towards mankind must exactly be proportioned to his conduct towards the Jewish nation. Let us therefore place God in common over them both; and there will be on the one side, the Jewish nation; and on the other, mankind: on the one side, Canaan, and a national prosperity;

on the other heaven and human happiness: on one side, a redemption from Egyptian servitude and national evils; on the other, a redemption of the whole human race from absolute evil: on the one side, national crimes atoned by national ceremonies, sacrifices, priests; on the other, sins expiated by the one universal sacrifice of Jesus Christ: on one side, national and temporary saviours, kings, prophets and judges; on the other, all this universal and eternal: on one side, the law, and every branch of it, adapted to a favourite nation; on the other, the everlasting gospel suited to all mankind.

It is impossible, therefore, that God can say anything to David, under the quality of king of this chosen nation, which he does not speak, at the same time, to Jesus Christ, as King of all the elect; and that in a truer and nobler sense. To each of them he speaks in a sense adapted to the nature of their respective kingdoms. Nor is this latter a bare accommodation of words, but the first and highest meaning of them, and which only, absolutely speaking, can be the true sense of God; the other being this sense, confined to a particular circumstance; in other words, an absolute truth, made history, and matter of fact. This is a principle, which shows, that far from denying the Christian application, I consider the literal and historical sense only as a kind of vehicle for it.

We have seen that through his Gospel, God calls us into a relation with himself as the Triune LORD in which he is the bountiful giver of all that is good for us for time and eternity. In Baptism by birth from above we enter this covenant of grace; in Confirmation we are strengthened by the Spirit, and we promise to be faithful as members of the Church of God and as the humble covenant partners of the LORD; and in the Daily Offices we recognize what this membership and partnership means through confessing our sins, praising the Lord our God, hearing his Word, and offering our petitions and intercessions to him.

Through hearing and meditating upon his Word and in the dynamic encounter with God which the Daily Office allows, believers enjoy communion with God through Jesus Christ, their Lord. This daily and continuing encounter is intimately related within the logic of faith and of liturgy to the unique encounter with God which he provides in "The Order for the Administration of the Lord's Supper." Holy Communion is the weekly, sacramental meal of the new covenant; it is the unique, spiritual food provided from heaven by the Lord our God for his covenant people on each Lord's Day as well as on special holy days (and indeed whenever they gather in his name and for his glory to celebrate the Eucharist). Yet it is a feast for which the covenant people of God must prepare so that they are truly ready to receive such supernatural and heavenly food. It is not intended to be "fast food" but "food" which is eaten after careful preparation.

The Communion is with the Father through the incarnate Son, Jesus Christ, who is the only Mediator between God and mankind, and by the power of the Holy Ghost. Only because the Son as true God took to himself from the Virgin Mary our human nature and flesh, and satisfied the demands of the law of God in our place—even to the extent of offering himself as the sacrifice for our sins—have we, as sinners, any right to approach God at all. In The Order for Holy Communion we are so marvelously united as believing sinners by the Holy Spirit with the exalted Lord Jesus, who died for us, that we are enabled to participate in and truly benefit from his full redemption, which covers both our bodies and souls.

In the Catechism we are taught that in this Sacrament "the inward part, or thing signified, is the Body and Blood of Christ, which are spiritually taken and received by the faithful." Further we learn that "the benefits whereof we are partakers in the Lord's Supper are the strengthening and refreshing of our souls by the Body and Blood of Christ as our bodies are strengthened and refreshed by the Bread and Wine."

## THE LOGIC OF FAITH

As put together by Archbishop Cranmer in 1549/52, the Lord's Supper has the same basic structure, the same logic of faith as the Daily Office. In the first part, called the Ante-Communion (based on the "Liturgy of the Catechumens" in the early Church), there is an introductory sequence of this logic of faith. The worshippers move on from the recognition before God of their sinfulness through hearing God's holy law and asking for mercy in two stages. First, they move to the hearing of the revelation and grace of God in the two readings (Epistle and Gospel) from the New Testament and the proclamation of good news in the sermon. Then, secondly, they move to the expression and responsiveness of faith in the Creed and the Prayer for the "whole state of Christ's Church." And after this Prayer, at least on the First Sunday in Advent, the First Sunday in Lent and on Trinity Sunday, the congregation begins its preparation to receive the Sacrament by hearing the Exhortation, beginning, "Dearly beloved in the Lord, ye who mind to come to the holy Communion.... "

In the second part, once called the "Liturgy of the Faithful," there is the same sequence but in a different and deeper way. "Ye who do truly and earnestly repent you of your sins ... " are invited to draw near with faith, confess their sins to God, and take the holy Sacrament so as to receive divine support and spiritual sustenance. Then follows the Absolution and the hearing of the comforting (comfortable) promises and assurances of God's grace to penitent sinners. This is followed by thanksgiving for salvation, faith responding to divine grace and celebrating that heavenly mercy. In the *Sursum Corda*, therefore, the forgiven, praising, covenant people of God lift up their hearts and give thanks as they are joined in the Holy Spirit to the heavenly choir who magnify and glorify the Name of the Lord our God. The thrice "Holy" cry is offered to the Father, the Son, and the Holy Ghost, one God.

Faith is now expectant, and Christian souls are ready to be fed by heavenly manna from the Table of the Lord. In the consecrated bread and wine, which is the sacramental body and blood of the Lord Jesus, who was crucified but is gloriously alive for evermore, God ministers to his covenant people. He feeds them spiritually as they are in union with himself in the Body of Christ with the gracious salvation which he has already proclaimed to them in the gospel words of assurance and mercy. Receiving the sacramental body and blood of Christ is thus the summit of responsive faith. Such faith unites believers in the Spirit with the Lord of glory so that what he is and possesses now in heaven is shared with his faithful people. Having been nourished and having been allowed to enter into intimate knowing/ communion with their Lord at his heavenly table, the covenant people of God then go forth into daily life to "continue in that holy fellowship and do all such good works as [God] has prepared for [them] to walk in." Thus Liturgy is for life: knowing God in common prayer and corporate worship becomes the basis of the daily vocation of serving God in the world.

Over the centuries the Cranmerian basic structure of the double and deepening logic of faith of this Service has been modified (some would say enriched) in the revisions of the Common Prayer Tradition. However, the basic biblical logic of personal confession of sin, the announcement to penitents of forgiveness and grace, and the response of faith to what God graciously offers in Jesus Christ by the Holy Spirit is still much in evidence in all editions of *The Book of Common Prayer* up to the Canadian Book of 1962. Before and since 1962, there has been a constant chorus of criticism of the Common Prayer Tradition accusing it of majoring too much on sin, guilt, and justification by faith through grace alone. This chorus is informed not by more profound Bible study and deeper knowledge of divine revelation, but rather by immature knowledge of the history of liturgy and corporate worship and by modern contemporary secular studies in the anthropological and social sciences. We need always to remember that human beings are not merely rebels against God who need to stop their rebellion and be forgiven, they are also diseased sinners who need an internal cure from the heavenly Physician and Saviour! They need to be lifted out of the power of the old epoch/age, which is dominated by sin and death, and placed into the new epoch/age in Christ wherein is everything that God has planned for them. Thus it is the new creation in Christ Jesus, not the old creation in original sin, which lies at the heart of this Service. It is the celebration of the new creation in, with, and by Christ in the presence and power of the Holy Ghost in the presence of God the Father.

## THE LECTIONARY: HEART OF THE PRAYER BOOK SYSTEM OF DOCTRINE

In the ancient Lectionary, the cycle of Epistle and Gospel lessons which has been in use in the Church of the West for over a millennium, the essential message of God's word to his covenant people is presented in an orderly and logical way. As the congregation of Christ's flock follows these lessons through the Christian Year, Sunday by Sunday and through Festivals, and gradually sees the pattern and content of them, it is led, step by step, into an ever deeper appreciation of Christian truth and the essentials of Christian life.

For the first half of the Year, from Advent to Trinity Sunday, the cycle of lessons printed in the Prayer Book presents the great, saving works of God in which the mind and heart of God are revealed in Jesus Christ: that is, those saving deeds in Christ by which the reconciliation and redemption of man are accomplished and the people of God are called to new life in the Holy Ghost, the Paraclete of Jesus Christ. Then, all this revelation and teaching, illumination and inspiration made known in these mighty works is wonderfully brought to a climax in the adoring contemplation of God, the Holy Trinity. In the Spirit, the congregation of Christ's flock is caught up in the Spirit to know the Father through the Son and by the Holy Ghost—One God, a Trinity in Unity and a Unity in Trinity.

Inspired by the heavenly vision, and being made by grace partakers of the divine nature, the stage is now set for the people of God to make progress in Christian maturity of life and sanctification of body and soul, as they take the liturgical journey from Trinity Sunday to the Sunday immediately before Advent. For the first half of the year, the celebration has been of God's character and deeds; for the second, the call is to draw certain practical conclusions from these Events and Truths. Not surprisingly, therefore, the first Lesson for the Sunday after Trinity is the divine love: "If God so loved us, we ought to love one another." The revelation of God's love, the divine charity, is the basis of the Christian commitment to the life of love. (See further, chapter ten below, "God is love.") In the many Sundays after Trinity the intent of the lessons is to show how the virtues and graces of the Christian life (= "the fruit of the Spirit") are based upon and derived from the revealed love, charity, and mercy of God. In hearing them, understanding and digesting them, the people of God are all set to manifest in their lives the love and mercy of God, and, in the context of the Eucharist, to be the better prepared to go to the Table of the Lord to be fed with heavenly manna.

SACRAMENT OF THE NEW COVENANT

There are accounts of the institution of the Lord's Supper in three Gospels

(Matt. 26:26ff; Mark 14:22ff; Luke 22:14ff) as well as by St Paul (1 Cor. 11:23ff). We learn from them that the new covenant, that is the new, everlasting relation of fellowship and communion between God and man in Christ Jesus, was inaugurated by the bloody sacrifice of atonement which Jesus offered in his death upon the Cross of Calvary. Thus at the Last Supper he referred to the cup of wine as "my blood of the new testament [covenant] shed for ... the remission of sins" and to the bread which he broke as "my body broken for you."

This means that the primary reference of the Liturgy of the Lord's Supper can be only the sacrificial, atoning death of Christ Jesus at Calvary, and what this Atonement achieved for God's creatures, who stand in need of being reconciled to him and redeemed by him. Certainly Jesus took the fruit of the old creation, the wheat-bread and the wine, and used them as the effectual signs and symbols of the new creation; but the emphasis is not upon the old creation as such but upon the new, the kingdom of God of the new age. Of this glorious future kingdom, to be known in full after the Second Coming of Jesus Christ in glory, the gathered church on earth experiences the first-fruits in this age, in anticipation of the total and never-ending fruit in the fullness of the life of the kingdom to come.

Being invited to the Lord's Supper and eating at his table is to receive a taste of the food of the kingdom of God to come. It is to be given a preliminary place at the heavenly Messianic banquet. It is to be fed now with that spiritual and heavenly manna which will sustain the life of the redeemed, new creation in heaven for all eternity. The body and blood of Jesus, the heavenly Lord who died for our sins and rose for our justification, are truly heavenly, nourishing food to our souls and bodies, for by them we are incorporated more fully and intimately into his mystical Body. We are joined to him as our Lord and Mediator, King and Physician, Master and Saviour. And in, through, and by him, we come to the Father. Yet this spiritual and heavenly banquet is open only to repentant, believing souls. There are dire warnings both given by Paul (1 Cor. 11:27ff.) and written into the three Exhortations provided for use in *The Book of Common Prayer* concerning coming to the Table of the Lord without having first made suitable spiritual and moral preparation.

Happily the Common Prayer Tradition does not fix one particular way of explaining how the risen and exalted Lord Jesus Christ, who once died for us, is actually present in the celebration of the Lord's Supper. Of course, he has promised always to be with his people: "Lo I am with you alway, even unto the end of the world," and so he is present through the Spirit, his

Paraclete or Comforter (John 14–16), at all church services with his gathered people. Nevertheless, there is a special, covenanted presence promised to the believing, faithful people of the new covenant when they meet at his holy Table to eat his body and drink his blood. In a manner which defies final description, he is specifically present in the breaking and eating of bread and the pouring and drinking of wine, for he makes them his own body and blood unto those who are united to him in faith and love. Those who come with penitent and believing hearts to his Table do not need to offer him an explanation of how the Sacrament works, or have an explanation offered to them. They know that it works for their salvation and that they increase in the knowing of their Lord, not by the exercise of their understanding, ingenuity, or magic, but by his supernatural grace.

Perhaps Queen Elizabeth I was not far wrong in her theology of the Eucharist in the following quatrain that she is reputed to have composed:

> He was the Word that spake it,
> He took the bread and brake it;
> And what that Word did make it,
> I do believe and take it.

Faithful reception at this Sacrament and this unique means of grace includes a basic, simple faith as is expressed here by the Queen.

Bearing this in mind, those who are walking with God and confessing Jesus as Lord in their daily lives ought to approach the Table of the Lord each Lord's Day. It is entirely appropriate that the Lord's people be at the Lord's Table on the Lord's Day, the day of resurrection and of the future kingdom of God. They should rejoice to be invited to attend his Messianic Feast on each anniversary of his Resurrection in order to know that their sins are forgiven, that they are reconciled to God in Christ, that unto them is given the taste and the promise of everlasting life, and that they have a vocation from God on this earth now in this sinful epoch to glorify their heavenly Father by their good works. Thereby the Liturgy is truly liturgy for life for they are sent forth from the Banquet to serve God in his world. Likewise, whenever possible the people of the new covenant should be present at his Table on the major feast days of the Christian Year (for which see chapter nine below).

Yet, it also must be noted that approaching the Table of the Lord is not to be undertaken lightly and easily (as in much modern Eucharistic practice), for it is the Table of the King of kings. The Eucharistic Feast is not a kind of religious fast food to be devoured as and when one feels like it, or custom requires.

# A COMPARISON

Though the *BCP* (1928) and *BCP* (1962) belong to the same Common Prayer Tradition, they present in their Services for Holy Communion two slightly differing forms. The Canadian Book may be traced back to the English *BCP* (1662) in a straight line. In contrast, the American edition of 1928 can be traced back to the English *BCP* (1662) only via the American editions of 1789 and 1892 and also via the input of the English Non-Jurors of the late seventeenth century and of the Scottish Episcopal Church of the eighteenth century. The major difference between the two is in the Prayer of Consecration.

The American Prayer addresses the Father in "the Oblation" in these words: "we do celebrate and make before thy Divine Majesty, with these thy holy gifts, which we now offer unto thee, the memorial thy Son hath commanded us to make." The key words are "which we now offer unto thee," which are not in the *BCP* (1662) or its successors. This clause comes from the Scottish Service of 1764. The thinking behind its inclusion is that there must be oblation in connection with remembrance. Cranmer had removed the oblation because of its association in the late medieval period with the idea of the Mass as a propitiatory sacrifice, offered to God for the removal of sin. The replacement of the act of oblation was intended to recover what was done in the early Church when the offering of the holy gifts to God was seen not as a propitiatory sacrifice but as the offering of prayer, praises, and the "holy gifts" of bread and wine.

Following the Oblation the American Prayer of 1928 has "the Invocation" wherein the merciful Father is asked "to bless and sanctify, with thy Word and Holy Spirit, these thy gifts and creatures of bread and wine." Here the Second and Third Persons of the One Godhead are understood to effect that gracious work whereby those who receive the consecrated bread and wine actually receive the Body and Blood of Christ. This invocation is not in the *BCP* (1662) and its direct successors.

There is one further difference to note. The Lord's Prayer is presented in *BCP* (1928) as the climax of the Prayer of Consecration and thus comes before the Prayer of Humble Access ("We do not presume ... "). In contrast the Lord's Prayer is said immediately after the Communion in the *BCP* (1662 & 1962).

Some would argue that the additions to the Common Prayer Tradition in the Scottish and American Books bring the Prayer of Consecration more into line with the earlier Liturgy of the Church before the medieval period in East and West, and thereby make it a more satisfactory Prayer. Others believe that the Cranmerian approach began a new tradition, that which may be called "Reformed Catholicism," which is wholly satisfying in and of itself and need not be changed.

## A SUNG EUCHARIST

There seem to be not a few churches which have a service of Holy Communion early on Sunday morning when there is no music and there is no singing. Here one may say that there is fellowship through speech, silence, symbol, and sacrament. In contrast, at the later service of the Holy Eucharist most churches have some singing and some music, where usually there are more people present and where there is an organist and perhaps a choir. The usual places where hymns are sung is in procession to begin the service, between the Epistle and Gospel, at the Offertory, during the administration of Communion, during the Ablutions and as a recessional. Where possible these should be chosen to fit appropriately into the movement and logic of the service, and they should help to raise human spirits God-ward.

In terms of the liturgy itself, there have been musical settings for centuries for the response to the reading of the Law of God, the Collect, the Epistle, the Gospel, the Creed, Sursum Corda, Sanctus and the Proper Preface, the Lord's Prayer and the Blessing. When they are used it is better to do a few of them well than to do the whole in a shoddy manner. Singing to the Lord is the purest form of address that man possesses, and so the knowing of the Lord in spiritual union will be intense when the singing is truly in the beauty of holiness. This singing unto the Lord is not in any way to be seen as a performance, but, rather, as an offering to God, the response of the Bride to the love of the Bridegroom, who calls her to his banquet. Again, it needs to explained that the music for the Order for Holy Communion does not have to be music from an earlier century; it can be contemporary, but whether new or old it must be of such a type that it actually serves the purpose of worshipping the Lord in spirit and in truth.

## REFLECTIONS

(i) The logic of faith of the Order for the "Administration of the Lord's Supper" requires for its full expression and development biblical preaching. And the Order for Holy Communion is the only service in the Prayer Book where a sermon is required. The homily is the divinely-appointed means of grace whereby God's Word addresses those who have gathered and brings them deeper in understanding and feeling to their Lord. So the sermon is hardly the place for a discussion of the latest politics or social problems: these can be considered at other times and in other places. Though there are many different ways of preaching, for by it God's Word comes through a human personality, yet there is only one basic content in preaching—a message from God and of God's salvation to God's people. It is a message from heaven addressed to earth; it is glad tidings of the kingdom of God addressed to the kingdoms of this world; it is the gospel of redemption addressed to needy sinners; it is a call of sanctification addressed to would-be saints.

(ii) Following medieval and Roman Catholic practice, the Canadian *BCP* (1962), unlike the *BCP* (1662) and the *BCP* (1928), includes between the Prayer of Consecration and the Prayer of Humble Access what has come to be called "the Peace". However, it is said in the context of the whole congregation kneeling and thus there is no possibility of people moving around to greet or hug friends. This stands in contrast to the way "the Peace" has come to be understood and practiced since the appearance of the new Books in the 1970s.

In the new Books "the Peace" is placed between the Ministry of the Word and the Celebration of the Sacrament and it is intended to be an important part of the Service. Normally people are encouraged to move about and greet one another in ways they deem appropriate. This is done in order, it is stated, to accord with ancient practice, as far as this is known. The Canadian *BAS* (1985) offers an explanatory note on what is "the Peace." It is "an encounter, a reconciliation, and an anticipation." As an encounter it allows the worshippers "to meet Christ in others"; as a reconciliation it dramatizes the injunction of Matthew 5:23–24 (to be reconciled to your brother before bringing your gift to the altar); and as an anticipation "it dramatizes the eucharist as a foretaste of the banquet of the kingdom" through the experience of peace and unity.

These are noble thoughts, but for their realization modern Eucharistic assemblies must compare favorably with those of the Early Church, whose practice of sharing "the kiss of peace" (Rom. 16:16; 1 Cor. 16:20; 2 Cor. 13:12; 1 Thess. 5:26 & 1 Pet. 5:14) was much more than "hello" or "how are you?" Too often today "the Peace" becomes *the* focal point of the Service, and is the place where people (out of the individualistic ethos of modern life) affirm one another, without apparently any reference to the teaching and demands of the Gospel of Christ. Many people obviously seem to enjoy the experience of greeting each other; however, whether it is appropriate or true to the Gospel as currently practiced is another matter. It surely ought to be done if and only if it truly makes a contribution to the purpose of the assembling together—to meet the Lord Jesus, to be one with his people, to hear his Word, and to be fed at his Table with his Body and Blood.

Cranmer was well aware that he had omitted the "peace be with you" which was in the Latin Mass that he revised (at the place where it is in Canada 1962); but he made good this omission by making the Blessing at the very end contain the giving of God's peace—for it begins as he composed it, "The peace of God which passeth all understanding...."

(iii) There is a great need in the parishes to recover a spirit of awe and reverence at and in this holy service. A celebration before God and with the Lord Jesus is not a secular event, but is the holy Lord calling his covenant people before him to share in his holy love. Certainly there is joy, abundant joy, at the Messianic Feast, but it is holy joy. Perhaps modern Anglicans should have fewer celebrations of Holy Communion in order to give themselves opportunity to revive the classic tradition of being able rightly to prepare for attendance at those they actually attend. Perhaps also modern worshippers need to think again about the way they dress and conduct themselves when coming to the Supper of the Lord. Does not a feasting with a King demand that guests dress in a way which honors him, rather than in a way that is appropriate for a leisure activity?

(iv) In modern times the discipline of fasting before receiving Holy Communion has gone into hiding, partly because Roman Catholic teaching and practice has become ever more lax in the West. There is no compulsion to fast before Communion; but there are powerful reasons at least to eat and drink only the minimum beforehand so that one's mouth and digestive system are truly ready to receive heavenly food: and, further, that one's energy is not being used up digesting a full meal in the stomach when it is needed for the demanding exercise of worshipping the Lord in the beauty of holiness. There are good reasons for fasting before Communion!

(v) The congregation of Christ's flock, which knows the Father through the Son by the Holy Ghost in worship, and especially in this Sacrament, will truly be prepared to see its vocation in God's world clearly and to have the will and strength to fulfill the same. So a people that knows the Lord and is known by him will be a caring people, a missionary-minded people, an evangelistic people, and a people whose good works glorify the Father in heaven. As one body and as members thereof, they are sent out into the world to love and serve the Lord their God and to love their neighbor as themselves.

## WISDOM FROM CHRISTOPHER SUTTON

In reading Anglican writers over the years I have noticed the great respect many had for the writings of Christopher Sutton, a canon of Winchester Cathedral. Here is an excerpt from his much read book, *Godly Meditations upon the Most Holy Sacrament of the Lord's Supper*, 1613.

This is the marriage feast of the King of heaven: the Banquet is spiritual, whose bread doth strengthen man's heart and whose wine doth inflame the soul with heavenly joy; and the meat thereof is the flesh of Christ, who says, "My flesh is meat indeed." This is that healthful food of angels sent down from heaven, having in it all delight and savoury sweetness. This is that fat bread which giveth pleasures for a king. This is the most plentiful bread of good nourishment above all that earth yieldeth. This is the bread of the offering of the first fruits. This is the bread signified as well in the cakes, which Abraham did set before the angels, as also in the shewbread; and this was likewise revealed in the bread and wine which Melchizedek brought forth. Lastly, this is the bread baked upon the coals in the strength whereof Elisha did walk forty days and forty nights unto Horeb, the mount of God. This is that tree of life, planted by the Almighty God in the midst of the earthly paradise, whose fruit being eaten would preserve bodily life. This is that Paschal Lamb without spot, by whose blood dabbed upon the two posts and the lintel of the door, the children of Israel were in times past delivered from the hand of the angel that smote the Egyptians. This is that kid which Manoah offered unto the Lord upon the stone. This is also that honeycomb which Jonathan, dipping the tip of his rod therein, did put to his mouth and his eyes were enlightened. This is also that large flowing stream of water which suddenly issued out of the rock after Moses had stricken it with his rod.

Come freely therefore to this most sweet Banquet of Christ Jesus wherein is promised unto thee most assured life and salvation … Oh therefore, faithful soul, if thou be unclean, come to the fountain of purity; if thou be hungry, come and feed of the bread of life which fadeth not and filleth the hungry soul with goodness. Art thou sick? This will be a most sovereign medicine for thine infirmity … Art thou sorrowful and in perplexity? This wine doth make joyful the inward man. Do many things trouble thee? Cleave fast to him who calmed the waves of the sea when they were troubled. Goest thou astray from the Lord and Master? Yet mayest thou walk in the strength of this meat, even to the Mount of God....

## THEOLOGY FROM SAMUEL SEABURY

Bishop Seabury has left us a well argued theology of the Holy Eucharist in his Discourse VI in *Discourse on Several Subjects* (vol.1. 1815). In this extract he explains the logic of the Prayer of Consecration of *BCP* (1789 & 1928):

At the time of the celebration, the officiating bishop or priest, first gives thanks to God for all his mercies, especially for those of creation and redemption. Then, to show the authority by which he acts, and his obedience to the command of Christ, he recites the institution of the holy sacrament which he is celebrating, as the holy evangelists have recorded it. In doing this, he takes the bread into his hands and breaks it, to represent the dead body of Christ, torn and pierced on the cross; the cup also, of wine and water mixed, representing the blood and water which flowed from the dead body of Christ, when wounded by the soldier's spear. Over the bread and the cup he repeats Christ's powerful words, THIS IS MY BODY, THIS IS MY BLOOD.

The elements being thus made authoritative representations, or symbols of Christ's crucified body and blood, are in a proper capacity to be offered to God as the great and acceptable sacrifice of the Christian Church. Accordingly, the oblation, which is the highest, most solemn, and proper act of Christian worship, is then immediately made. Continuing his prayer, the priest intercedes with the Almighty Father to send upon them (the bread and wine) the Holy Spirit, to sanctify and bless them and make the *bread* the *body* and the *cup* the *blood* of Christ—his spiritual life-giving body and blood in power and virtue; that, to all the faithful, they may be effectual to all spiritual purposes. Nor does he cease his prayer and oblation, till he has interceded for the whole catholic church, and all the members of it; concluding all in the name and through the merit of Jesus Christ, the Saviour.

The Eucharist being, as its name imparts, a sacrifice of thanksgiving, the bread and wine, after they have been offered or given to God, and blessed and sanctified by his Holy Spirit, are returned to the hand of his minister to be eaten by the faithful, as a *feast upon the sacrifice*—the priest first partaking of them himself, and then distributing them to the communicants; to denote their being at peace and favour with God, being thus fed at his table, and eating of his food; and also to convey to the worthy receivers all the benefits and blessings of Christ's natural body and blood, which were offered and slain for their redemption.

For this reason the Eucharist is also called the communion of the body and blood of Christ; not only because, by communing together, we declare our mutual good will and our unity in the church and faith of Christ; but also, because, in that holy ordinance we communicate with God through Christ the Mediator, by first offering, or giving to him the sacred symbols of the body and blood of his dear Son, and then receiving them again, blessed and sanctified by his Holy Spirit, to feast upon at his table, for the refreshment of our souls; for the increase of our faith and hope; for the pardon of our sins; for the renewing of our minds in holiness, by the operation of the Holy Ghost; and for a principle of immortality to our bodies, as well to our souls.

From this consideration, the necessity of frequently communicating in the Holy Eucharist evidently appears.

It is the highest act of Christian worship; a direct acknowledgment of God's sovereignty and dominion over us and over all his creatures. It is the memorial of the passion and death of our dear Redeemer, made before the Almighty Father, to render him propitious to us, by pleading with him the meritorious sufferings of his beloved Son, when he made his soul an offering for sin. It is a sensible pledge of God's love to us, who, as he hath given his Son to die for us, so hath he given his precious body and blood, in the holy Eucharist, to be our spiritual food and sustenance: and as the bread of this world frequently taken is necessary to keep the body in health and vigour; so is this bread of God, frequently received, necessary to preserve the soul in spiritual health and keep the divine life of faith and holiness from becoming extinct in us.

## 9

We live in space and time, dependent always upon the Lord our God for life. For us day succeeds day, month succeeds month, and year succeeds year. We cannot escape time. In contrast, God, who is the Creator of space and time, is above and beyond space and time. He is eternal and infinite Spirit, and upon him space, time, and all creatures are dependent. Not only is our God present unto us through space and time, but he has also acted decisively for us by revealing himself in space and time. The center of this revelation is the Incarnation of the eternal Son of God, who took to himself our human nature and brought salvation, reconciliation, and redemption to the world by what he did for us as Jesus, the crucified and exalted Messiah. We rejoice that God acted for us and our salvation in the specific space of Palestine, and in the chronological time, when Herod and his sons were kings under the protection of the Roman Empire.

The Church Year, beginning on Advent Sunday, exists to facilitate our knowing God as his adopted children and covenant partners, as we focus upon Jesus Christ in dependence upon the presence and ministry of the Holy Ghost in the Church. As we exist in space and time the Christian Year brings us into constant contact with different dimensions and aspects of the one Mystery, even our Lord Jesus Christ. *Mystery*, the word for God's saving activity in Jesus, is the word Paul often uses. To appreciate the Church Year as dependent upon, relating to and expressing the Mystery, we shall benefit by noting its rich meaning in the Letters of Paul.

MYSTERY & MYSTICAL

The Greek word, *mysterion*, occurs twenty-seven times in the New Testament, and of these twenty occur in the Letters of Paul. Where *mysterion* occurs, we find that it is in association with verbs which point to revelation from God or proclamation of the gospel of God. Thus *mysterion* is God's secret, long kept by him and then disclosed by him through the Holy Ghost to the apostles. In their proclamation of the Gospel and in their teaching concerning Christ Jesus, this secret is told to all who believe. Believers learn and receive the *mysterion* in order to know the God of mercy and grace in whom they believe; and in particular, by this *mysterion* they know the Lord Jesus Christ as they exist in personal, spiritual union with him.

Paul's reflections upon the *mysterion* begin as he compares God's wisdom and the wisdom of this world in 1 Corinthians 1–2. It is in the Cross, the saving, atoning, redeeming and reconciling activity of the living God in Christ Jesus, that true wisdom is to be found. While the preaching of the Cross appears as foolishness to the secular-minded, to those whose eyes God has opened it is the revelation of heavenly wisdom and the power of salvation. Thus Paul explains: "We speak the wisdom of God in a *mystery*, even the hidden wisdom, which God ordained before the world unto our glory" (2:7).

In the apostolic preaching of the Gospel, the mystery which has been kept a secret by God is proclaimed to the world. Paul makes this clear in the way he ends the Letter to the Romans:

> Now to him that is of power to stablish you according to my gospel, and the preaching of Jesus Christ, according to the revelation of the **mystery** which was kept secret since the world began, but now is made manifest, and by the scriptures of the prophets, according to the commandment of the everlasting God, made known to all nations for the obedience of faith: To God only wise, be glory through Jesus Christ for ever. Amen. (16:25–27)

He also asked for prayer that he would preach this *mystery*: "Continue in prayer ... that God would open unto us a door of utterance to speak the mystery of Christ, for which also I am in bonds" (Col. 4:3; see also Eph. 6:19).

By the Gospel God's saving activity in the death of Jesus is revealed: the long-kept secret is manifested. But there is yet more to the *mystery*, and Paul gives us the details. He tells the church in Ephesus "how that by revelation God made known unto me the *mystery* ... which in other ages was not made known to the sons of men, as it is now revealed unto his holy apostles and prophets by the Spirit: That the Gentiles should be fellow-heirs, and of the same body, and partakers of the promise in Christ by the gospel: whereof I was made a minister...." (3:4–6). The Gospel of God creates a new humanity in which there will be the reconciliation of Jew and Gentile in one Body, the Body of Christ. This contrasts with the situation under the old covenant when all God's people were of Jewish stock, but it is what God always had in mind. This *mystery* is revealed in the Gospel, for by his Cross Christ creates a new people, a new creation, and a new covenant.

There is yet more to the *mysterion*. God's plans call for the internalizing of his grace within the souls of all his new people. Writing to the church in Colosse, Paul speaks of the *mystery* which has been hidden from ages and generations but is now made manifest to his saints and continues: "To whom God would make known what is the riches of the glory of this *mystery* among the Gentiles, which is Christ in you, the hope of glory" (1:27). The indwelling of the Holy Spirit by whom Christ is present in the soul is an aspect of the *mystery*. This indwelling is first encountered in the effects of the divine activity in the Cross of Christ. No wonder Paul can cry out: "I am crucified with Christ, nevertheless I live; yet not I, but Christ liveth in me; and the life I now live in the flesh I live by the faith of the Son of God, who loved me and gave himself for me" (Gal.2:20). It is from this aspect of the *mystery* that we get the true meaning of *mystical*, the experience of God the Holy Trinity in the soul—knowing the Father, through the Son and by the Holy Ghost.

In terms of God's purpose for his creation, there is also the cosmic dimension of the *Mysterion*. In the saving deed of Calvary is the power and promise of cosmic regeneration. To the church in Ephesus, Paul writes: "God hath abounded toward us in all wisdom and prudence, having made known unto us the mystery of his will ... that in the dispensation of the fullness of time, he might gather together in one all things in Christ, both which are in heaven and which are on earth...." (1:9–11). God's secret, revealed in the Gospel and made possible by what happened at Calvary, is to sum up all things in Christ. By him all things were created, and to him all things will return for their perfection.

Finally, Paul speaks of "the great **mystery**" which is "concerning Christ and the Church" (Eph. 5:32). The intimate union of the people of the new covenant with the Lord Jesus is the great *mysterion*! The Church is the Bride, and the Lord Jesus is the Bridegroom, and they are bound together in *mystical* union.

We may summarize what has been said in one short sentence from Paul: "Great is the *mystery* of godliness" (1 Tim. 3:16). It is to this *mystery* or *secret* of God, revealed in the Gospel, that the Church Year points; and in this mystery God's covenant people, as the Bride of Christ (who is Lord of the Year), partake during their keeping of and living within the Church Year. Finally, the *mystery* of the revelation and impartation of the divine love and charity is the very basis of the Eucharistic Lectionary, wherein is a practical system of teaching on this Love (see further chapter ten).

Obviously the Church does not keep the Christian Year simply in terms of remembering past events and drawing appropriate moral and spiritual conclusions from them. The Church, as it were, places itself in past time and is there in union with the righteous remnant of Israel, with the Lord Jesus himself, and with his apostles and disciples. This time may be called liturgical time for it is in the narrative and drama of the liturgy that the saving revelation and events are read, rehearsed, proclaimed, taught and assimilated. It is as though we were there with Mary and Joseph in the stable, with the wise men from the East in Bethlehem, at the river Jordan when Jesus was baptized, in Jerusalem for Holy Week, there with the disciples when the risen Lord appeared and when he ascended, and there in the upper room when the Holy Ghost descended.

## SUNDAY

In the Ten Commandments God's covenant people were told to "remember the Sabbath day, to keep it holy" (Ex. 20:8). Ever since Jesus Christ rose from the dead on the first day of the week, Christians have called this day "the Lord's Day" (Rev. 1:10) and kept it as their day of worship. So instead of the seventh day, Christians meet to hear God's Word and celebrate the Lord's Supper on the first day of the week. They have done this from the very beginning, as the Gospel of John (20:19*ff.*) and the Acts of the Apostles (20:7*ff.*) make clear. It is the day when the *mystery* is declared in the Gospel and received in the Sacrament.

In biblical teaching, days, and the week of seven days, belong to the creation of space and time by the Lord God. As the first chapter of Genesis declares, God made the world in six days and rested on the seventh to contemplate what he had made. So the seventh day is the Sabbath; and its fulfillment, according to the Letter to the Hebrews, is the sabbath-rest for the people of God as they engage in contemplating God's glory in the kingdom of heaven in the age to come. The fact that Christ rose on the first day and that his Church keeps this day for the worship of Almighty God in his name is a biblical way of proclaiming that by and through the redeeming work of Jesus, God has begun a new creation. Further, the first day is also, on a seven day week, the eighth day, and the resurrection of Jesus on this day points to a new start, a new epoch, a new age, and a new world centered on the Lord Jesus Christ, the risen and exalted Saviour. You may have noticed that some baptismal fonts have eight sides to declare this truth and to tell the baptized that they enter a new creation by their incorporation into Christ.

While Sunday is always the Festival of the Resurrection, each day is special, for it is a gift from God and an opportunity to meet with him and to serve him. It is a great comfort to know each morning, midday, and evening that the Lord our God does not change and that his boundless mercy is constant. We can always rely upon him even if we cannot trust our own feelings and thoughts. In the Daily Office we encounter the *mystery* through the written Word. The Old Testament points forward to Christ crucified for us and for our salvation, and the New Testament proclaims the *mystery* in all its manifold meaning and application to our lives. In meditation we ponder and consider the *mystery,* and in contemplation we encounter the *mystery* "Christ in you, the hope of glory." This discipline of prayer is sustained by the monthly cycle of psalms as we pray in and with Christ who is the *Mystery* himself.

## CHRISTMAS

There are two major moments in the Christian Year, Easter and Christmas. In connection with each Festival there are special festivals and holy days before and afterwards.

Though there is no certainty that Jesus was born on December 25, the Church has kept this as the date of his birth for a long time. It is the celebration of the Incarnation, the eternal God becomes Man, the Second Person of the Holy Trinity takes to himself human nature. The One, who would make known by his Cross the secret kept hidden through all ages, is born of the Virgin Mary. So at this season,

> *It is very meet, right and our bounden duty to give thanks unto thee, O Lord, Holy Father, Almighty, Everlasting God, Because thou didst give Jesus Christ thine only Son to be born as at this time for us; who, by the operation of the Holy Ghost, was made very man, of the substance of the Virgin Mary his mother; and that without spot of sin, to make us clean from all sin.*

We may speak of the mystery of the Incarnation, not only because it is beyond our understanding that God became Man, but also because the Incarnation was for a purpose, the salvation of the world at the Cross. By the *mysterion* we are made "clean from sin."

The four Sundays of Advent (*adventus* = coming) exist to turn our thoughts and affections towards the Lord Jesus Christ in heaven who came into this world, "born of a woman and born under the law" (Gal. 4:4) and who will return to this world "to judge the living and the dead." Only with a whole view of Christ and a full knowledge of him, his identity and work, can there be true joy and gladness at Christmas. And, further, during Advent the faithful gain a sense of the *mystery* which is the summing up of all things in Christ at the end of the age when he comes to judge the living and the dead (Eph. 1:9–10).

Only when the festival of the Nativity is seen in the light of the kingdom of God of which Jesus is the King can there be genuine celebration of the grace of God. For unless this festival is approached and experienced in the Spirit, and with the light of biblical truth, it can so easily be sentimentalized and its saving grace and meaning lost. In terms of knowing God, the festival is a marvelous opportunity to contemplate 1) "the weakness of God" as seen in the helpless baby's dependence upon Mary, his mother, and 2) the condescension of God, not merely to our level but to our lowest level, in order to save us. "Thou shalt call his name Jesus for he will save his people from their sins" (Matt. 1:21).

Other events described in the Gospels and specifically related to the birth of Jesus have been given dates in relation to Christmas Day. On March 25 is *The Annunciation of the blessed Virgin Mary*, nine months before Christmas; on January 1 is *The Circumcision of Christ*, eight days after his birth and on February 2 is *The Presentation of Christ in the Temple*, according to Jewish law. Finally on June 24 is *The Nativity of John the Baptist*, who was born several months before Jesus.

Also intimately related to Christmas and the Incarnation of the Son of God are the twelve days of Christmas which run from Christmas Day to Epiphany, which in the West celebrates "the Manifestation of Christ to the Gentiles." In terms of the *mysterion*, the Epiphany is of great importance because an aspect of God's long-kept secret is, as Paul puts it, "that the Gentiles should be fellow-heirs, and of the same body [as the Jews] and partakers of his promise in Christ by the gospel" (Eph. 3:7). The visit of the Gentile astrologers to worship the new-born King was an important pointer in this direction.

EASTER

In the period before, during, and after Easter the faithful are particularly conscious of the *mysterion*; they are brought into vital contact with the Lord Christ, who died for their sins, rose for their justification, was exalted for their redemption, and ever lives to make intercession for them.

The date of Easter varies from year to year because it is fixed with respect to the Jewish Passover, and this, in turn, is based on the phases of the moon. Easter Day is always the Sunday after the full moon that occurs on or after the Spring equinox on March 21. Thus Easter cannot be any earlier than March 22 or later than April 25.

The two all-important days are Good Friday, the day of the crucifixion, and Easter Sunday, the day of the resurrection. Before Good Friday is the period of Lent and Holy Week, and after Easter Day are the forty days to the Day of Ascension and then there are a further ten days to Whit-Sunday or Pentecost. One may think of the *mysterion* in relation to the whole period, and one may also think of aspects of the *mysterion* in relation to specific days and period.

Casting our minds over the whole period, we can see how there is the preparation through testing of Jesus for his final suffering and sacrificial death, and his descent into Hades. Here God is reconciling the world to himself in his beloved Son in a way which defies all the wisdom of the world (1 Cor. 1-2). *The mystery hidden in God is at last revealed for the salvation of the world.* By raising Jesus from the dead and exalting him to his right hand in heaven, the Father almighty declares that there is truly a gospel for the world: the apostles have a *mystery* to proclaim to the whole world and it is good news. By sending the Holy Spirit at Pentecost to unite his covenant people to his beloved Son, as his Body, the Father reveals another dimension to the *Mysterion*. Baptized believers as the new covenant people of God are the Bride of Christ, united to him by the Holy Ghost; in *mystical* union and in each person the Holy Ghost dwells, granting thereby *mystical* experience of God to him or her.

All these themes are to be found in the Collects, Epistles, and Gospels for this period. Therefore, for the believer this holy time provides a wonderful opportunity, in Paul's words, for the expression of this desire: "that I may know Christ, and the power of his resurrection and the fellowship of his sufferings, being made conformable unto his death" (Phil. 2:10).

On Ascension Day the liturgy not only celebrates another Resurrection appearance but also the actual ascending of the Lord Jesus into the Shekinah, the cloud of glory (the symbol of God's presence in heaven). Liturgically, this ascent has been celebrated by the extinguishing of the Paschal Candle, which has been lit since Easter Day. Ten days after the Ascension and after experiencing holy and joyful expectancy, the Church arrives at the feast of Pentecost and, with the disciples in the upper room, awaits the descent of the Holy Ghost (Acts 2). With this Event, the celebration of the mighty works of God in Jesus Christ and by the Holy Ghost is concluded. But there is one more Feast to celebrate, and this is the Feast of the Holy Trinity. In the divine Events celebrated in the Festivals from Christmas to Whitsuntide, there has been a wonderful revelation of the nature and character of God. He is the Father, together with his only-begotten Son and his Holy Spirit. God is a Trinity in Unity and a Unity in Trinity, and he is to be adored and served.

And the name of the Holy Trinity gives the title to the rest of the Sundays of the Christian Year, the long season of Trinity, wherein the faithful have space and time to reflect upon the name, nature, revelation and works of the Blessed, Holy and Undivided Trinity, and also to enjoy communion with the Father through the Son and by the Holy Spirit. The God who is Three in One and One in Three is Creator and Revealer, Redeemer and Judge; and many aspects of his relation to mankind are brought before our attention in this period in the appointed Collects, Epistles, and Gospels, which direct the people of God to look to Jesus Christ. They see in him the nature and character of God as well as the source of their salvation, so that in following and serving him they can glorify his Father, whom they call, "Our Father." They pray,

> Stir up, we beseech thee, O Lord, the wills of thy faithful people; that they, plenteously bringing forth the fruit of good works, may of thee be plenteously rewarded; through Jesus Christ our Lord. Amen.

This is the last prayer on the lips before Advent Sunday arrives and the whole cycle of knowing God through the Church Year begins again. And there is another opportunity to grow in grace and the knowledge of God.

Finally, we need to remember that within the yearly cycle are found holy days on which the Virgin Mary, the Apostles, Saints, and Martyrs are remembered (often called red letter days because they were printed in red in old Prayer Books). These holy ones were faithful to the *mysterion* and in them was reflected the *mystery* of "Christ in you the hope of glory" (Col. 1:27). From them, we learn what it is to know, love, and serve our Lord Jesus Christ.

SMALL WORDS WITH AN IMPORTANT FUNCTION

The relation of the faithful to the Lord Jesus and thus to the God and Father of our Lord Jesus Christ in worship and life may be usefully understood by noticing the use of three different prepositions—*through, in,* and *with*—all of which are used in an "odd" way and by this oddness point to their special, indeed unique, use in Christian teaching. In the keeping of the Christian Year this relation is particularly obvious.

In Liturgy, we often hear the words "through Jesus Christ" at the ending of collects and prayers. Here the Church is recognizing (a) that there is one Mediator between God and Man, and (b) that this Man, the Lord Jesus Christ is the Way, the Truth, and the Life, and (c) that no one comes to the Father except through and by him. Since he is, as the God-Man, One Person made known in two natures, the Church approaches the Father in prayer and praise, in service and mission, through the Lord Jesus Christ. There is no other way. Thus the normal structure of prayers and collects, and especially the Eucharistic Prayer, is that of addressing the Father through the Son and with/by the Holy Ghost.

One of the favorite expressions of the apostle Paul is "in Christ," and this also is found in the Liturgy. By this phrase is meant that each baptized faithful believer is a member of his Body, united to him by the Holy Ghost and thus, as it were, contained within or incorporated into his human nature. The Church is joined to Christ so closely and intimately that it is "in him." Because of this the Church, as accounted and reckoned by God for the merits of Jesus Christ, is righteous (justified), sanctified (set apart for God and addressed as "saints"), and even glorified (for Christ Jesus is glorified in heaven). In daily reality on earth the Church and each member is seeking to become in practice what God reckons it/he is because of the saving work and presence of Jesus. The Church, and each member thereof, are seeking to become in practice what they are reckoned to be by the Father as being "in Christ." Therefore, they are able to partake of his fullness, of his graces, virtues and gifts within the movement and content of the Christian Year. It is noteworthy that in the Prayer of Consecration, the Celebrant prays that the people of God may be "made one body with him [Christ], that he may dwell in us and we in him."

To be "with Christ" is more than being alongside him in meditative thought; it is being in step with him, united in mind, heart, will, and direction with his step. In the drama of the Liturgy, the Church is with him in the Christian Year from his conception and birth, through his infancy and childhood, into manhood, and thus into his Ministry, Passion, Crucifixion, Burial, Resurrection, Ascension, Exaltation, Session, and Second Coming. And outside the Liturgy the Church has the vocation of walking with him daily in the world, as members of his Body indwelt by the Holy Ghost and thereby walking in the Spirit to love and serve their Head and Lord.

*Lord of all power and might, who art the author and*
*giver of all good things; Graft into our hearts the love of*
*thy Name, increase in us true religion, nourish us with*

*all goodness, and of thy great mercy keep us in the same;*
*through Jesus Christ our Lord. Amen.*
(Seventh Sunday after Trinity)

## CHANGES IN MODERN LITURGY

Modern liturgists have made changes not only to the structure and content of services of worship, but also to titles and arrangements of the Christian Year. These changes have practical consequences, as we shall now see.

Of these, the most important is the expanding of the title "Easter" to cover the whole fifty days from Easter Day itself, the Day of Resurrection, to Pentecost, and to call this period "the great fifty days." Thus the Sundays in this period from Easter Day itself up to the Sunday immediately before Pentecost all have the name "Easter"—Easter 1, 2, 3, 4, 5, 6, & 7. This contrasts with the traditional Christian Year in the West, where there is Easter, the first Sunday after, the Second Sunday after, and so, on until Ascension Day (40th day), and then the Sunday after the Ascension, which is the Sunday immediately before Whit-Sunday (Pentecost).

In the new arrangement there is an obvious reduction in the importance of the Feast of the Ascension of our Lord on the 40th day. In practice it is often neglected, or it is transferred to the following Sunday as "the Seventh Sunday after Easter," and thus it loses its distinctive character. This new order particularly suits those for whom the Resurrection is not truly a bodily resurrection but rather some kind of spiritual resurrection. And, theologically, it serves to leave Christ, as it were, raised from the dead but still on or around the earth. He is not ascended on high, crowned the King of kings and Lord of lords in his glorified human nature; and he is not present in heaven as our Prophet, Priest and King.

In the West, it was always the custom until the 1970s at the Feast of the Ascension on the fortieth day after Easter, to snuff out the Paschal Candle which had been alight since Easter Day. This signified that Christ has ascended into the cloud of glory and thus into heaven, to prepare a place for his people (see the Collect, Epistle and Gospel in the *BCP* 1928). The modern custom is to keep the Candle lit until Pentecost, which could suggest that, if there is an ascension, it occurs as the Holy Ghost descends on the fiftieth day.

Modern liturgists claim ancient practice for their commitment to the Easter of fifty days, and in this claim they have some justification. What, however, they do not consider and explain to modern worshippers is that, when the Feast of the Ascension was introduced in the fourth century and gradually became a universal Feast, then the fifty days remained but not as a straight fifty, as it were; it became forty plus ten, and this fact led to the naming in the West of the Sundays from Easter Day to Whit-Sunday/ Pentecost in the way that they are found in the old Latin Missal and in the classic English *Book of Common Prayer*. The clear advantage of the forty plus ten is that it follows the biblical pattern, and also actually celebrates the Ascension of Jesus, for if he is not ascended then everything he did for us and for our salvation has a question mark by it!

Now to one further point. The Christian Year in *the Book of Common Prayer*, as was noted in the remarks on the Eucharistic Lectionary in chapter 8, naturally divides at Trinity Sunday, which is the climax of the first part and the launch-pad for the second part. The arrangement of naming the Sundays as "Sundays after Trinity" goes far back into medieval times. In contrast, because the "great fifty days" is made the center of things in the new prayer books, the year is divided at Pentecost, and thus Sundays after it are within the "Season of Pentecost" (see the *BCP* 1979). Naming the period from Pentecost to Advent Sunday as "the Season of Pentecost" also has ancient precedent, but it cannot be imposed on *the Book of Common Prayer*, because of the centrality of Trinity Sunday as the climax of the portrayal of the mighty works of God for the redemption and reconciliation of the world to himself, and as the beginning of the practical application of these truths in the life of the church and each member thereof.

# GOD IS LOVE

## 10

Genuine Christians do not confess that love is God; they confess that God, as the Almighty Lord, is Love. In fact, the early Christians took a Greek word, *agapē*, and made it their special word for speaking of the love that is in God, the love by which God reaches out to save sinful creatures and the love which he places in their souls as he saves them from sin. Truly blessed are those who know and experience that their God is not only loving but Love. The celebration of the divine charity is the basic message, as we have seen, of the ancient Eucharistic Lectionary which takes so large a part of the content of *The Book of Common Prayer*.

## BIBLICAL REFLECTION

The Epistle for the first Sunday after Trinity in *The Book of Common Prayer* is 1 John 4:7–21. Twice in this passage we hear one of the briefest but most important statements of the whole Bible: *God is love.* John wrote: "He that loveth not knoweth not God: for God is love. In this was manifested the love of God towards us, because that God sent his only begotten Son into the world, that we might live through him. Herein is love, not that we loved God, but that he loved us, and sent his Son to be the propitiation for our sins." To believe and confess that God is Love, in the manner and spirit of St John, is to sum up in three words what we learn about the one, living God from the whole of his self-revelation recorded in Holy Scripture.

However, to state that the Holy Trinity, the Lord our God, is Love is not to deny what is said in both the Old and New Testaments of his wrath against sin and evil, and of his chastising of his covenant people when they forsook him and worshipped idols. Further, to say that God is Love is to say that the almighty God, who made the whole universe out of nothing and maintains it moment by moment, he truly is Love. To affirm that God is Love is to say that the God who guided the patriarchs into Egypt and allowed their descendants to become slaves, he is love. Also to confess that God is Love is to say that the God who sent the tribes of Israel from Palestine into captivity and exile in Assyria and Babylon where many perished, he is Love. Further, to confess that there is a hell and that God will send there those who totally reject his offers of salvation by grace is to claim *that* is Love. Finally, to state that God is Love is to say that God the Father, who caused the Messiah, Jesus of Nazareth, to suffer, to be crucified and to descend into hell, for us and for our salvation, he is Love.

The God who is Love is the God of justice and righteousness. Further, anyone who tries to drive a wedge between the wrath and the love of God is not being instructed by the Holy Scriptures in his thinking. The God who punishes the disobedient is truly the God who is Love. This biblical approach to the character of God is a problem for us if we think or feel (as so many seem to do) that all love is God, rather than if we begin with God and confess with St. John that God himself is Love. Perhaps great harm has been done in the Church in recent times by seeking to describe God in sentimental terms of what is considered to be love amongst and in human beings. Certainly the Common Prayer Tradition is very clear on this point and directs worshippers always to God's self revelation in sacred Scripture for an understanding of what is genuine love, compassion, mercy, and grace.

It is very important for us to grasp this point because the fact that God himself is Love is the basis of the divine command that we love God and one another. In the Epistle for the first Sunday after Trinity the second occurrence of "God is love" is as follows: "God is love; and he that dwelleth in love dwelleth in God and God in him ... We love him because he first loved us ... he who loveth God loves his brother also." Therefore, it is extremely important that we know God and in knowing God know him as Love in order that from and in that Love we are able to love our fellow men, especially our fellow believers in Christ.

Such is the prayer that Anglicans have offered to God on the Sunday immediately before Lent (Quinquagesima):

> O LORD, who hast taught us that all our doings without
> charity [love] are nothing worth; send thy Holy Ghost, and
> pour into our hearts that most excellent gift of charity, the
> very bond of peace and all virtues, without which whoso-
> ever liveth is counted dead before thee: Grant this for thine
> only Son Jesus Christ's sake. Amen.

Following this Collect, the Epistle is the great hymn of love written by Paul in 1 Corinthians 13. "Though I speak with the tongues of men and of angels, and have not charity [love], I am become as sounding brass, or a tinkling cymbal."

It is important that we notice that before John wrote "God is love" he wrote "God is light." He said: "This is the message which we declare unto you, that God is light, and in him is no darkness at all" (1:5). On this basis, John proceeded to call upon his readers to "walk in the light as God is in the light" and thereby to have fellowship one with another and to experience the power of the forgiving, cleansing blood of Jesus Christ in their hearts and in their fellowship. Not to walk in the light (that is, being enlightened and illumined by God's self-revelation and presence) is to walk in darkness (that is, "enlightened and illumined" by the ethos and standards of this sinful age and world).

Bearing this in mind we have to say that "God is love" means "God is holy love" and "God is righteous love." God as love is not love as divorced from absolute purity and righteousness: rather, his love is pure, holy, and righteous love. God's love will, therefore, chastise and punish, for God is not in the business of making people happy who will not seek for holiness and purity of life. However, to confess that "God is love" and "God is light" is to believe that God's love and holiness find expression in everything (with no exceptions) that God says and does. To know God as the Lord is to know God as the One who is entirely consistent in his character and his dealings with us. We learn what is divine love by contemplating the deeds and words of the living God for our salvation, sanctification, and redemption, and then by experiencing the work of the Holy Ghost in our lives.

There are some marvelous descriptions of the love of God in the writings of Paul apart from 1 Corinthians 13 cited above. In Romans 5 and 8 the apostle waxes eloquent concerning the presence of the love of God in the human soul: "the love of God is shed abroad in our hearts by the Holy Ghost which is given unto us" (5:5). Then he asks the rhetorical question: "Who shall separate us from the love of Christ?" (8:35) and comes quickly and eloquently to the conclusion that nothing whatsoever in the whole invisible or visible created worlds "shall be able to separate us from the love of God which is in Christ Jesus our Lord."

Love, pure love, which is of God, begins within the Godhead and is the dynamic, holy essence of the relation of the Father to the Son and the Son to the Father, the relation of the Father to the Holy Ghost and the Holy Ghost to the Father, and the relation of the Son and the Holy Ghost to each other. God is Love as a Trinity of Persons. In holy Love the Father eternally begets the Son and spirates the Holy Ghost: thus the Holy Trinity is a Trinity of Love. From the Father through the Son and by the Holy Ghost all Love flows both into creation and into redemption. As St John stated it: "God so loved the world that he gave his only begotten Son...." (John 3:16).

Finally, from Paul's writings we may note the prayer request of the apostle in Ephesians 3:14ff., where he kneels in prayer to the Father in heaven and longs that "Christ may dwell in your hearts by faith: that ye, being rooted and grounded in love, may be able to comprehend with all saints what is the breadth, and length, and depth, and height: and to know the love of

Christ which passeth knowledge, that ye might be filled with all the fullness of God." One may doubt whether the theme of this book can be better expressed than Paul has done for us here. To know God experientially is to be filled with the love of God; but, it is also at the same time to recognize and to understand that God who is Love is greater than our highest thoughts and beyond our loftiest contemplation of him. For the God who is present as the Holy Ghost (as the Spirit of Christ) in his Church and with his covenant people is the God who is also utterly transcendent, beyond space and time, and glorious in his transcendence, holiness and Majesty.

THE DIVINE LOVE IN LITURGY

The Common Prayer Tradition captures this great theme of the holy love of God in a variety of ways. God's love in creating and maintaining the world is affirmed as an expression of his goodness. There is a full and always moving presentation of the love of God manifested in Jesus Christ, in his Incarnation, mission, passion, death, resurrection and exaltation. Likewise the sending by the Father through the mediation of the Son of the Holy Ghost to the Church is presented as a further manifestation of God's love, the love provided to be the holy principle and content of the souls, hearts, minds and wills of those who believe on the name of the Lord Jesus.

So we may join James I. Packer in explaining God's love in this way: "God's love is an exercise of his goodness towards individual sinners whereby, having identified himself with their welfare, he has given his Son to be their Saviour, and now brings them to know and enjoy him in a covenant relation" (*Knowing God*, 1973, p. 111). From the beginning of this book, I have sought to explain not only that we know God because he first chooses to know us; but, also that our knowing of each other in fellowship is always within the covenant relation, which he establishes. How this works in the Common Prayer Tradition with respect to God as holy love and pure goodness we must now briefly survey.

Baptism and Confirmation exist as Sacraments because of the holy love of God. There is a Gospel to proclaim since God so loved the world that he gave his only-begotten Son to die for our sins and to be raised for our justification. Messengers are sent into the world by the Lord Jesus because in his love he has provided salvation for all who will believe upon his holy Name. "Go ye therefore, and teach all nations, baptizing them in the name of the Father and of the Son and of the Holy Ghost: teaching them to observe all things whatsoever I have commanded you" (Matt. 28:19–20). Divine Love calls sinners, and in the love of God they believe and are baptized into his covenant to enjoy his steadfast, faithful love.

The Daily Office exists as the appointed means of being encountered daily by God because of his holy love and goodness. God mercifully calls his covenant people to be with him, to recognize his Majesty, to confess their sins, to hear his Word, to receive his forgiveness and salvation, to petition him and to intercede with him and to know him as the Holy Trinity, the LORD. In this daily discipline, centered upon God's self-revelation recorded in Scripture and celebrated in Psalms and Canticles, there is a growing awareness of the height and depth, the breadth and length of the holy love of God. The soul gradually lays aside all conceptions of love based on human insights and is drawn into the mind of Christ to share his understanding and experience of the divine love.

Through reading and meditating upon Scripture in the Daily Office, God's covenant people are truly taught the nature and meaning, as well as the practice of, real love, the love of God. Their prayers, flowing from this formative reading, become more and more the prayers of love for the brethren and expressions of the love of God shed abroad in their hearts by the Holy Ghost given unto them. It may be said that the Litany is a total expression of loving disciples addressing the Lord of love, Jesus Christ, in petition and intercession.

The Holy Communion is pre-eminently the Sacrament of the holy love of God. Here is the Love which forgives, cleanses, justifies, sanctifies, unites to Christ, and feeds with heavenly manna at the heavenly table. This is the holy love so splendidly described in the Proper Prefaces for Christmas Day, Easter Day, Ascension Day, Whit-Sunday and the Feast of the Holy Trinity. And it is the love which as goodness and mercy is recognized and celebrated in the Prayer of Consecration:

> Almighty God, our heavenly Father, who of thy tender mercy didst give thine only Son, Jesus Christ, to suffer death upon the Cross for our redemption; who made there (by his one oblation of himself once offered) a full, perfect, and sufficient sacrifice, oblation and satisfaction for the sins of the whole world....

In the words "full, perfect, and sufficient" we hear what love achieved and what we never could have earned by our merit, and certainly do not deserve. Then, having been fed by God at the Holy Table of his Son, the people of God cannot but pray:

> Almighty and ever living God, we most heartily thank

> *thee, for that thou dost vouchsafe to feed us, who have duly*
> *received these holy mysteries, with the spiritual food of the*
> *most precious Body and Blood of thy Son our Saviour Jesus*
> *Christ; and dost assure us thereby of thy favour and good-*
> *ness towards us; and that we are very members incorporate*
> *in the mystical body of thy Son....*

Being fed on heavenly manna is only part of the revelation of the love of God. There is the inner assurance of the covenant favor, grace, and tender mercy of God for believing sinners; and there is communion and union with the Lord Jesus Christ, wherein human spirit speaks to Spirit—"that he may dwell in us and we in him." This is living knowledge indeed!

In the service known as "The Order for the Visitation of the Sick," God's tender mercy, love, and goodness are the divine realities which make this event meaningful and necessary. Love is expressed in the opening saluta-tion: "Peace be to this house, and to all that dwell in it." Divine love is then assumed in everything which follows. The purpose of the service is that the sick person may hear God's gracious promises and truly know God and be known by him. Whether the sick person is to recover or whether he is to die, the aim is to make sure that he is in a right relation with God and knows that God the Father is Love and that Christ loves him now. Thus after Psalms and Collects the priest says:

> *The Almighty Lord, who is a most strong tower to all*
> *those who put their trust in him, to whom all things in*
> *heaven, in earth, and under the earth, do bow and obey;*
> *Be now and evermore thy defence; and make thee know*
> *and feel, that there is none other Name under heaven given*
> *to man, in whom, and through whom, thou mayest receive*
> *health and salvation, but only the Name of the Lord Jesus*
> *Christ. Amen.*

In sickness and in pain, it is truly good to know and feel the promises and presence of the Lord Jesus Christ.

In "The Form of the Solemnization of Matrimony" the word love occurs as the key word in the relation of the two persons in marriage. "Wilt thou love her?" and "Wilt thou love him?" are asked, and each also promises "to love and to cherish" until parted by death. It is obvious here that "love" is primarily a commitment of the person to a particular kind of living together and caring throughout all possible circumstance, good and evil—"for better for worse, for richer for poorer, in sickness and in health." Love here is much more than sexual activity, affections and emotions. It is an act of the will determined to do the utmost good to and for the other person in this relation of matrimony. And the theological context for marriage is the heavenly marriage between Christ as the Bridegroom and the Church as his Bride, a relation brought into being because Christ loved the Church and gave himself up for her on his Cross at Calvary (Ephesians 5:21–33).

Finally, we note that the service for "The Burial of the Dead" is based wholly on the doctrine of the love of God in Jesus Christ which pardons sin and gives the gift of eternal life to all who receive the Gospel. The first words are the wonderful promise of Jesus Christ: "I am the resurrection and the life ... " God's comfort is communicated to those who mourn through familiar Psalms and through the reading of 1 Corinthians 15, the classic New Testament passage on the resurrection of the dead and the glorious life with Christ in the age to come. In an optional Collect the continuing knowing of God both by the departed and the living is recognized:

> *O Almighty God, the God of the spirits of all flesh, who by thy voice from heaven didst proclaim, Blessed are the dead who die in the Lord; Multiply, we beseech thee, to those who rest in Jesus, the manifold blessings of thy love, that the good work which thou didst begin in them may be perfected unto the day of Jesus Christ. And of thy mercy, O heavenly Father, vouchsafe that we, who now serve thee on earth, may at last, together with them, be found meet partakers of the inheritance of the saints in light; for the sake of the same thy Son, Jesus Christ our Lord.*

Both the dead and the living await both the resurrection of the dead and what has been termed the beatific vision, the beholding of the glory of God in the face of Jesus Christ, Incarnate God, and thus being totally immersed in the love of the Holy Trinity.

FEAR AND LOVE TOGETHER

Perhaps to our surprise, the prayers within *The Book of Common Prayer* bring together "fear" and "love" as natural companions. "Make us to have a perpetual fear and love of thy holy Name," is the petition in the Collect for Trinity 2. In the Offices of Instruction the duty of the baptized believer towards God is stated as, "to believe in him, to fear him, and to love him with all my heart, with all my mind, with all my soul, and with all my strength." In the Old Testament, especially in the Book of Deuteronomy, there is a clear linking of this double duty of both fearing and loving God. Israel is required by the Lord God, "to fear the Lord your God, to walk in all his ways, to love him, to serve the Lord your God with all your heart and with all your soul … " (10:12–13). In the Psalter and the Book of Proverbs the fear of the Lord is both the beginning of wisdom and of knowledge [of divine things] (Prov. 1:7; 9:10; Psalm 111:10).

And though it is not so prominent as in the Old Testament in terms of usage, the duty to fear the Lord our God is clearly stated in the New Testament. In fact, it is taken for granted as the essential background for true worship, genuine love, and service of the Father through the Son with the Holy Ghost. Did not Mary, the mother of Jesus, proclaim that God's mercy "is on them that fear him throughout all generations" (Luke 1:50)? Does not an angel in heaven proclaim, "Fear God and give him glory, and worship him" (Rev. 14:6*ff*; see also 15:4 & 19:5)? In fact, the Letter to the Hebrews declares that the prayers of Jesus himself were heard by his Father because of his godly fear (Heb. 5:7).

Fear, as a godly affection of the soul, is a profound sense of reverence and awe felt by the genuinely penitent believer as he, a sinner, is aware both of the presence of the One true and living God, who is perfect in holiness and righteous, and of his duty to love and serve him, despite his sinfulness. Without such fear, there can be no true worship, since the presence of godly fear enables worship genuinely to be addressed to his Majesty, to the all-glorious, the all-righteous, and the all-pure God. Without such fear, there can also be no genuine love of God as the one true God, for to love and adore him in his Triune Being and in his attributes, we must have a profound sense of dread, awe, and reverence. Thus fear is the beginning of the knowledge/knowing of God, and it is indispensable both in corporate worship and in personal devotions.

Fear is necessary on earth because it is wonderfully present in heaven. The fear present in heaven is the thrilling of beatific joy, the trembling of an ecstatic adoration. This fear in the redeemed people of God does not tremble because its blessedness is insecure, or because there is any cloud between God and itself. It trembles because of the tremendous Majesty which it sees, because of the amazing familiarity of communion to which it is admitted, and because of the vehement intensity of love to which it is raised. All through the vastness of heaven, except within the tranquility of God himself, the Blessed, Holy Trinity, this rapturous fear is to be experienced.

## CONCLUSION

Finally, with many others I want to state that I always feel deeply moved when I join in the familiar but profound prayer called "A General Thanksgiving:"

> *Almighty God, Father of all mercies, we thine unworthy servants do give thee most humble and hearty thanks for all thy goodness and loving-kindness to us, and to all men. We bless thee for our creation, preservation, and all the blessings of this life; but above all, for thine inestimable love in the redemption of the world by our Lord Jesus Christ; for the means of grace, and for the hope of glory. And, we beseech thee, give us that due sense of all thy mercies, that our hearts may be unfeignedly thankful; and that we show forth thy praise not only with our lips but in our lives, by giving up ourselves to thy service, and by walking before thee in holiness and righteousness all our days; through Jesus Christ our Lord, to whom, with thee and the Holy Ghost, be all honour and glory, world without end. Amen.*

When these words become truly the prayer in the mind-in-the-heart of God's covenant people, it may be said of them not only that they know the Lord but also that they are known by the Lord our God. With St. Paul all faithful Christians want to exclaim: "I count all things but loss for the excellency of the knowledge of Christ Jesus, my Lord" (Phil. 3:8). The highest and greatest of all knowledge, that knowing which is excellent, is knowing God as the God whose face and ears are turned toward believing sinners. In knowing the Son, the congregation of Christ comes to know the Father through the presence of the Holy Ghost, and knowing God, the Father, the Son, and the Holy Ghost, the people of God have eternal life, even as they are known by God himself.

> *The Peace of God, which passeth all understanding, keep your hearts and minds in the knowledge and love of God, and of his Son Jesus Christ our Lord: And the Blessing of God Almighty, the Father, the Son and the Holy Ghost, be amongst you, and remain with you always. Amen.*

This proclamation and presentation in Scripture of this love of God is at the very heart of the Prayer Book system of worship and teaching, Christian maturity and sanctification, for it is the basic content of the Eucharistic Lectionary.

The Prayer Book Society of the USA exists to commend the use of the historic *Book of Common Prayer* primarily in its American edition (1928), but also in its English (1662) and Canadian (1962) editions.

The Society seeks to keep the 1928 edition in print for use in the USA. It also publishes books and pamphlets and produces compact disks to assist people to appreciate and understand the classic Prayer Book.

For more information, call 1-800-PBS-1928 and ask for a free copy of the magazine *The Mandate.*